$3
Meals

$3 Meals

Feed Your Family Delicious, Healthy Meals
for Less than the Cost of a Gallon of Milk

Ellen Brown

The Lyons Press
Guilford, Connecticut
An imprint of The Globe Pequot Press

This book is dedicated to my wonderful family, Nancy and Walter Dubler; Ariela Dubler; Jesse Furman; Ilan, Mira, and Lev Dubler-Furman; Lisa Cerami; and Josh Dubler. With all my love and thanks for your support.

To buy books in quantity for corporate use
or incentives, call **(800) 962–0973**
or e-mail **premiums@GlobePequot.com.**

The Lyons Press is an imprint of The Globe Pequot Press.

Text design: Sheryl P. Kober

Library of Congress Cataloging-in-Publication Data is available on file.

ISBN 978-1-59921-607-2

Printed in the United States of America

10 9 8 7 6 5 4 3 2 1

Contents

Here are the fundamentals of how to prepare a $3 meal; it comes from careful planning and strategic shopping. The chapter contains the foundation to learn how to trim the grocery budget.

It's not just the dinner entree that eats up the budget; it's all those ancillary foods such as salad dressings, sauces, and stocks. This chapter contains delicious ways to save money on condiments and components.

Thick and hearty soups are satisfying to the soul as well as the stomach, and when using homemade stocks they are merely $1 or so a serving—so you can splurge on some other meal that week. There are a few vegetarian soups, as well as ones made with all forms of protein.

While crustaceans like shrimp and crab are too pricey to be included within the scope of this book, there are delicious ways to prepare fish that are inexpensive. And there are also many great dishes to be made from our old friend, canned tuna fish.

The focus of this chapter is on the whole bird, not just its premium-priced boneless breast. There are recipes for the sum of its parts, as well as great creations made with leftover chicken and turkey. Lean ground turkey dishes are also well represented.

Meltingly tender pot roasts and beef stews, a few richly flavored dishes made with ground lamb and ground beef, and all things porcine—including sausage and ham—are celebrated with the recipes in this chapter.

Chapter 7: Vegetarian with Verve

Pasta, legumes, grains, and vegetables ranging from delicate to hearty star in this chapter. These dishes comprise an international collection of recipes that can be made both quickly and inexpensively.

Chapter 8: Bakery Basics

The increase in the cost of flour, and everything made from it—including bread and baked goods—represents an important part of the spike in food costs. The convenience of buying a loaf of bread will never be replaced, but the recipes in this chapter give options for treats that can be made for pennies.

Preface

There is an answer to combating the meteoric rise in food costs—it's called home cooking. It's not a new answer. It's one that has been around—and flourished—for the many centuries before Americans' four food groups devolved into frozen, delivered, eat out, and take-out.

What's cooking? It's the aroma perfuming the air from a chicken roasting with herbs in the oven on a lazy Sunday afternoon, or the fragrance of garlic and cheese coming from a pot of thick and hearty Bolognese sauce simmering on the stove. Cooking can be the yeasty smell of bread dough rising in a warm corner of the kitchen, or it can be the sight of a bubbling pot of stew simmering on the stove. Cooking, and filling your house with the sounds and smells of food being prepared, will definitely stretch your food budget; it will also bring more than monetary rewards to your life.

That's where this book comes in; it gives you recipes for how to cook inexpensive and nutritious meals in a time-efficient manner. You'll find that frugal and fresh can go hand in hand, especially after I've given you some tips on how to shop and cook so that no food is ever wasted.

Cooking food at home was how people ate for generations. In the decades following the end of World War II, however, "progress" became equated with how large a distance one could create from actual food preparation. As author Nora Ephron quipped, "My mother was a good recreational cook, but what she basically believed about cooking was that if you worked hard and prospered, someone else would do it for you." Her mother was hardly alone.

This "someone" was rarely a cook hired to work in the house; it was the manufacturer of canned or frozen foods. White sauces to moisten casseroles were replaced by cans of "cream of something soup"; the depth of flavor foods achieved from being made with long-simmered stocks was long forgotten as cans of all sizes lined the pantry; and frozen entrees grew from the small section of chicken pot pies and TV dinners, presented in sectioned aluminum foil trays, to entire supermarket aisles.

In fact, it's possible to trace Americans' attitudes towards cooking sociologically by examining the configuration of space in houses, and the size of the freezer compartment in refrigerators. Gathering a large family around a dining room table, or dinner parties for friends, gave way to open space living and fold-up trays so that the TV dinners could be eaten more easily in front of the TV set.

The small freezer unit of refrigerators in the 1960s, intended to keep ice and ice cream, grew by the start of the twenty-first century to a frozen cavern equal in size to the warmer unit for refrigerated foods. Americans had chosen convenience as the primary ingredient in their cooking. And for some, this was by necessity, as more and more women entered the work force. "Beat the Clock" was no longer just a television program; it was the way millions of cooks felt entering the kitchen after a long day's work, and trying to feed a hungry family within minutes.

It was also during this era that tried-and-true methods of parents and grandparents teaching children and grandchildren how to cook disappeared, and we entered an era of culinary illiteracy. People may have eaten pies on Thanksgiving, but chances are no one at the table knew how easy it was to make a tender and flaky homemade crust for the pie.

And some of this illiteracy was the result of the expansion of our food horizons. Few Americans, unless of Italian parentage, knew how to cook pizza—now an American staple—and gathering ingredients for Hispanic and Asian cooking proved a challenge until recently. So the prospect of enjoying these lusty "foreign" foods lured Americans out of their kitchens and into restaurants.

Open restaurant kitchens became a form of entertainment for diners, many of whom rarely saw people actually cooking. People considered it baking if a cake was created from a box of mix rather than purchased from a bakery; the concept that a cake could start with a recipe was almost foreign.

But all of this is changing. One reason is the rise in food costs, which have increased at a greater rate from 2007 until now than at any time in American history. As a general rule it is safe to say that the more a food is processed, the more expensive it becomes. Carrot sticks are more expensive than whole carrots that need peeling and cutting; preseasoned rice or stuffing mix is more expensive than adding seasonings to the base ingredient. And there's no reason to use these value-added products once you learn that it takes but minutes in the kitchen to do it yourself—and come out with a superior product, too.

The other reason why people are returning to cooking is the desire to stop eating the chemicals listed on food labels, and return to eating nutritious food. To achieve both goals, I hope you enjoy cooking the recipes in this book, and make cooking a part of your life.

Mid-twentieth-century writer A. J. Liebling wrote that "a good meal in troubled times is always that much salvaged from disaster." So save money, and feed your soul as well as your body.

—Ellen Brown
Providence, Rhode Island

Acknowledgments

While writing a book is a solitary endeavor, its publication is always a team effort. My thanks go to:

Ed Claflin, my agent, who had faith in the various iterations of this project, as well as for his constant support and great sense of humor.

Eugene Brissie, of The Lyons Press, for his faith in me and my ideas.

Ellen Urban, of The Lyons Press, editor extraordinaire, for her guidance and help all through the production process, and Jessie Shiers for her eagle-eyed copy editing.

My many friends who shared their culinary wisdom and tips for saving money.

Tigger and Patches, my furry companions, who personally endorse all fish and seafood recipes.

Introduction

This book is about tempting your taste buds, and helping you get delicious meals on the table with little effort—and few funds. It's true—you won't find any recipes here for lobster or filet mignon. But you won't miss these lavish foods because the foods you're eating have such great flavor, and a good blending of colors and textures to excite your eyes as well as your palate.

You'll find that budget is hardly synonymous with boring. The recipes in this book are for great American foods, and foods from cuisines that are increasingly popular options in this country. These dishes have vibrant flavors, but they're not made with exotic ingredients that cost a lot of money and that you might not use again.

Budget is also not synonymous with time-consuming. There isn't a recipe in this book that takes more than 20 minutes of your attention. Not that all the food is *ready* in 20 minutes, but for any amount of time beyond that magic number, the food is doing its own thing—marinating, cooking, cooling, chilling—while you can read a book or make another part of the meal. And there are some dishes that are on the table in a matter of minutes.

What you'll learn reading—and cooking from—this book is how far your finite food budget can stretch. The goal of *$3 Meals* is an ambitious one; this small amount of money—less than the cost of a large fast food burger or a slice of gourmet pizza—is for your *whole meal!* That includes the greens for your tossed salad and the dressing with which it's tossed. It includes the pasta or rice you cook to top with a stew or sauce. So unlike many books that promise cost-conscious cooking, this book shows you how to achieve savings beyond the entree. You'll learn how easy it is to bake breads and muffins for a fraction of the cost of foods found in bakeries.

The foundation of *$3 Meals* is all the tricks I've learned in professional kitchens—including my own catering kitchen. Professional cooks learn to minimize waste; wasted food translates to lower profit. That means that the onion peels and celery leaves that you might be throwing into your compost bin or garbage can now become an asset because you'll have them frozen to make stocks. And you'll know you have succeeded in waste-free cooking when, at the end of the week, there's nothing in the refrigerator to throw away! That's quite a feeling of empowerment, and along the way you've been eating like royalty on a peon's budget.

In addition to eating wonderfully, you'll also be eating more healthfully. It may not be by accident that *convenience* and *chemical* start with the same letter. Chemicals are what convenience foods are all about; they are loaded up with them to increase their shelf life, both before and after being opened. The recipes in this book don't contain such unhealthy ingredients as trans fats and high-fructose corn syrup, which can be hidden in processed foods, too.

One of the rules of economical cooking is that the more processed a food is, the more expensive it is. These recipes are made with foods that are ingredients; at one time they grew from the earth, walked upon it, or swam in its waters. The most processing that has taken place is the milk of animals having been transformed into natural cheeses. So when you're cooking from *$3 Meals*, you're satisfying your body as well as your budget.

There are a few ingredient compromises made to trim costs; however, these shortcuts trim preparation time, too. This is the first book I've written in which I used bottled lemon and lime juice in recipe development rather than freshly squeezed juices from the fruits themselves; I discovered it took a bit more juice to achieve the flavor I was after, but with the escalated cost of citrus fruits this was a sacrifice that I chose to make. The same is true with vegetables; many of these recipes call for cost-effective frozen vegetables rather than fresh. For vegetables such as the chopped spinach added to a soup or casserole, or the peas added to many dishes, using frozen produce doesn't affect the quality of the finished recipe.

I've also limited the range of herbs and spices specified to a core group of less than a dozen. There's no need to purchase an expensive dried herb that you may never use again.

On the other hand, there are standards I will never bend. I truly believe that unsalted butter is so far superior to margarine that any minimal cost savings from using margarine was not worth the trade-down in flavor. Good quality Parmesan cheese, freshly grated when you need it, is another ingredient well worth the splurge. You use very little of it, because once grated it takes up far more volume than in a block, and its innate flavor is far superior.

The same is true for using fresh parsley, cilantro, and dill. While most herbs deliver flavor in their dried form, these leafy herbs do not. Luckily, they are used so often that they are inexpensive to buy and don't go to waste—especially with the tricks I'll teach you on how to freeze them.

The other direction I frequently give that may seem like a "splurge" is lining pans with heavy duty aluminum foil. To me, the few pennies it costs is truly worth it in the time it saves to clean the pan. Time is money, too, and I would rather spend a bit more money to have more time to relax.

Chapter 1:
Strategies for Shopping and Cooking

Can you relate to this scene? It's 6:15 p.m., and you're just leaving the office. What are you going to do about dinner? How about linguine with white clam sauce? That can be on the table in less than 20 minutes, and you know the recipe in your head—not the quantities, but the basic ingredients. So you rush to the supermarket and can check out in the express line; that's good. But you're so hungry that you buy a bag of chips, too, and nibble them in the car. Then you arrive home. Darn. You just bought Parmesan cheese because you forgot that you had a hunk in the house. And come to think of it, the last time you made white clam sauce you did a double batch, so there's a full pint already in the freezer. Damn!

If you just saw yourself cursing, you're not alone. This scenario is played out by millions of Americans daily. Next to housing and auto expenses, Americans spend the largest percentage of their net income on food. While the percentage—about 14 percent—is less than in many other countries, it's still a chunk of money.

Planning and shopping are the cornerstones to trimming the fat out of your food bills, and you'll learn how to do both in this chapter. As the illustration was meant to demonstrate, it's impossible to keep within a food budget if you're stopping for small lists on a regular basis and impulse buying, too.

THE WEEK'S MASTER PLAN

The most important step to cost-effective cooking is to decide logically and intelligently what you're going to cook for the week. That may sound simple, but if you're in the habit of deciding when you're leaving work at the end of the day, chances are you've ended up with a lot of frozen pizza or Chinese carry-out. While this section on how to plan is very detailed, it really takes but minutes to compile your master plan once you've gotten in the habit.

The first step is to get into a frugal frame of mind. You're out to save money on your food budget, but not feel deprived. You're not going to be eating a bowl of gruel like Oliver Twist. You're going to be eating the delicious dishes in this book. With your same frugal mentality, think about where your food budget goes beyond meals at home. Couldn't you brew coffee and take it to work rather than spend $10 a week at the coffee cart? And those cans of soft drinks in the vending machine are four times the cost of bringing a can from home. Some friends started a "lunch club" at work to replace the $5 to $7 a day spent at restaurants sitting with each other. Each day one person brought enough lunch for four, and on the fifth day they went out. These steps alone can save up to $40 a week per adult.

Next, look at the week, and what activities are listed. How many nights will you actually be home? Are there any guests invited for any meals? How about the kids? Do they have activities that mean that the family won't be eating dinner together? Is there a sporting event on television that everyone will want to see, so eating may be on laps instead of a table? These are all questions to ponder before putting pen to paper.

The third step is to shop in your own house first. Look and see what's still in the refrigerator, and how that food—which you've already pur-chased and perhaps also cooked—can be utilized. Let's say you roasted a chicken a few days earlier, but it's not enough to feed the family for a second night. How about some chicken enchiladas? Or chicken cro-quettes? You've got little bags or containers of many leftovers; there's the cabbage leftover from the corned beef, lots of string beans, and plain pasta. What to make? You've got most of the ingredients for a hearty, main-course soup.

Now look and see what foods you have in the freezer. Part of savvy shopping is stocking up on foods when they're on sale; in fact, sales of free-standing freezers have grown by more than 10 percent during the past few years, while sales of all other major appliances have gone down. And with good reason—a free-standing freezer allows you to take advantage of sales.

But preparing food for the freezer to ensure quality is important. Never freeze meats, poultry, or seafood in the supermarket wrapping alone. To guard against freezer burn, double wrap food in freezer paper or place it in a heavy plastic bag. And always mark the purchase date on raw food and the date when frozen on cooked items, and use them within three months.

Also, part of your strategy as a cook is to do it only a few nights a week; that means when you're making recipes that can be doubled—like a pasta sauce or stew—you make larger batches and freeze a portion. Those meals are "dinner insurance" for nights you don't want to cook. Those are the nights that you previously would have brought in the bucket of chicken or the pizza, and spent more money for less nutrition.

The other factor that enters into the initial planning is looking at your depletion list, and seeing what foods and other products need to be purchased. A jar of peanut butter or a bottle of dishwashing liquid might not factor into meal plans, but they do cost money so they have to be factored into your budget. Some weeks you might not need many supplies, but it always seems to me that all of the cleaning supplies seem to deplete the same week.

So there's the "old business" part of the planning process. Now it's time to consider the "new business."

SAVVY SHOPPING

It's a new world out there. You're going to the supermarket and you're going to buy what's on your list. Here's the first rule: stick to that list. Never go shopping when you're hungry; that's when non-essential treats wind up in your basket.

The next time you are at the market, have a pad and pen with you. Take note of what is located where, such as "baking supplies (flour, sugar, chocolate chips) in aisle 2," and create a master form for your shopping list according to the layout of your market. Divide a sheet of paper into three columns, starting with the meats, fish and other protein, and then make listings for dairy products and shelf-stable pantry items by aisle number. After a few times, this system becomes so familiar that you will probably not be referring to your master guide.

Supermarkets are almost all designed to funnel traffic first into the produce section; that is the last place you want to shop. Begin with the proteins, since many items in other sections of your list relate to the entrees of the dinners you have planned. Once they are gathered, go through and get the shelf-stable items, then the dairy products (so they will not be in the cart for too long), and end with the produce. Using this method, the fragile produce is on the top of the basket, not crushed by the gallons of milk.

The last step is packing the groceries. If your grocery store gives you the option of packing them yourself, place items stored together in the same bag. That way all of your produce can go directly into the refrigerator, and canned goods destined for the basement will be stored in one trip.

BARGAIN BASICS

Every grocery store has weekly sales, and those foods are the place to start your planning for new purchases. And almost every town has competing supermarket chains that offer different products on sale. It's worth your time to shop in a few venues, because it will generate the most savings. That way you can also determine which chain offers the best store brands, and purchase them while you're there for the weekly bargains. Here are other ways to save:

- **Clip those coupons.** And use them! The best deal you can find is a coupon for an item that is being offered on a "buy one, get one free" promotion in the supermarket. Large companies publish coupons in every Sunday newspaper, and other companies send them at bulk rate with your mail delivery. You can save substantially by spending some time looking at the coupons. I found a $5 off coupon for a premium cat food my finicky cats liked in a local paper, which cost 50 cents. It was worth it to buy four copies of the paper; I spent $2 but I then netted an $18 savings on the cat food.

- **Find bargains online.** It's difficult for me to list specific Web sites because they may be defunct by the time you're reading this book, but there are hundreds of dollars worth of savings to be culled by printing coupons off of Web sites, and for high end organic products, it's the only way to access coupons. One I use frequently is www.couponmom.com, and I also look for the coupon offers on such culinary sites as www.epicurious.com. Also visit manufacturers' Web sites; they offer both coupons and redemption savings.

- **Find coupons in the store.** Look for those little machines projecting out from the shelves; they usually contain coupons that can be used instantly when you check out. Also, don't throw out your receipt until you've looked at it carefully. There are frequently coupons printed on the back. The cashier may also hand you other small slips of paper with your cash register receipt; most of them are coupons for future purchases of items you just bought. They may be from the same brand or they may be from a competing brand. Either way, they offer savings.

- **Stock up on cans.** Even if you live in a small apartment without even a basement storage unit, it makes sense to stock up on canned goods when they're on sale. The answer is to use every spare inch of space. The same plastic containers that fit under your bed to hold out of season clothing can also become a pantry for canned goods.

- **Shuffle those cards.** Even if I can't convince you to clip coupons, the least you can do for yourself is take the five minutes required to sign up for store loyalty cards; many national brands as well as store brands are on sale only when using the card. While the current system has you hand the card to the cashier at the checkout, that will be changing in the near future. Shopping carts will be equipped with card readers that will generate instant coupons according to your purchasing habits. I keep my stack of loyalty cards in the glove box of my car; that way they don't clutter my purse but I always have them when shopping.

- **Get a bargain buddy.** There's no question that supermarkets try to lure customers with "buy one, get one free" promotions, and sometimes one is all you really want. And those massive cases of paper towels at the warehouse clubs are also a good deal—if you have unlimited storage space. The answer? Find a bargain buddy with whom you can split large purchases. Many friends and I also swap coupons we won't use but the other person will. Going back to my example of the cat food savings, there were dog food coupons on the same page, so I turned them over to a canine-owning friend.

LEARN YOUR OPTIONS

The well-informed shopper is the shopper who is saving money, and the information you need to make the best purchasing decision is right there on the supermarket shelves. The shelf tag gives you the cost per unit of measurement. The units can be quarts for salad dressing, ounces for dry cereal, or pounds for canned goods. All you have to do is look carefully.

But you do have to make sure you're comparing apples to apples and oranges to oranges—or in this example, stocks to stocks. Some stocks are priced by the quart, while others are by the pound.

- **Check out store brands.** Store brands and generics have been improving in quality during the past few years, and according to *Consumer Reports*, buying them can save anywhere from 15 to 50 percent. Moving from a national brand to a store brand is a personal decision, and sometimes money is not the only factor. For example, I have used many store brands of chlorine bleach and have returned to Clorox time and again. But I find no difference between generic corn flakes and those from the market leaders.

- **Compare prices within the store.** Many foods—such as cold cuts and cheeses—are sold in multiple areas of the store, so check to see if there is a variation in price between alternate locations. Sliced ham may be less expensive in a cellophane package shelved with the refrigerated foods than at the deli counter because no labor is involved in its cutting.

- **Buy the basics.** When is a bargain not a bargain? When you're paying for water or you're paying for a little labor. That's why even though a 15-ounce can of beans is less expensive than the same quantity of dried beans (approximately a pound), you're still better off buying the dried beans. One pound of dried beans makes the equivalent of four or five cans of beans. In the same way, a bar of Monterey Jack cheese is much less expensive per pound than a bag of grated Monterey Jack cheese. In addition to saving money, the freshly grated cheese will have more flavor because cheese loses flavor rapidly when grated. And pre-cut and pre-washed vegetables are truly exorbitant.

WASTE NOT, WANT NOT

We're now going to start listing exceptions to all the rules you just read, because a bargain isn't a bargain if you end up throwing some of it away. Remember that the goal is to waste nothing. Start by annotating your shopping list with quantities for the recipes you'll be cooking. That way you can begin to gauge when a bargain is a bargain. Here are other ways to buy only what you need:

- **Don't overbuy.** Sure, the large can of diced tomatoes is less per pound than the smaller can. But what will you do with the remainder of the can if all you need is a small amount? The same is true for dairy products. A half-pint of heavy cream is always much more per ounce than a quart, but if the remaining three cups of cream will end up in the sink in a few weeks, go with the smaller size.

- **Ring that bell!** You know the one; it's always in the meat department of supermarkets. It might take you a few extra minutes, but ask the real live human who will appear for *exactly* what you want. Many supermarkets do not have personnel readily available in departments like the cheese counter, but if there are wedges of cheeses labeled and priced, then someone is in charge. It might be the deli department or the produce department, but find out who it is and ask for a small wedge of cheese if you can't find one the correct size.

- **Buy from the bins.** Begin buying from the bulk bins for shelf-stable items—like various types of rice, beans, dried fruits, and nuts. Each of these departments has a scale so you can weigh ingredients like panko breadcrumbs or couscous. If a recipe calls for a quantity rather than a weight, you can usually "eyeball" the quantity. If you're unsure of amounts, start by bringing a 1-cup measure with you to the market. Empty the contents of the bin into the measuring cup rather than directly into the bag. One problem with bulk food bags is that they are difficult to store in the pantry; shelves were made for sturdier materials. Wash out plastic deli containers or even plastic containers that you bought containing yogurt or salsa. Use those for storage once the bulk bags arrive in the kitchen. Make sure you label your containers of bulk foods both at the supermarket and, if you're transferring the foods to other containers, at home so you know what they are, especially if you're buying similar foods. Arborio and basmati rice look very similar in a plastic bag, but they are totally different grains and shouldn't be substituted for each other.

- **Shop from the salad bar for tiny quantities.** There's no question that supermarkets charge a premium price for items in those chilled bins in the salad bar, but you get exactly what you need. If you don't see how you're going to finish the $4 pint of cherry tomatoes, then spend $1 at the salad bar for the handful you need to garnish a salad.

SUPERMARKET ALTERNATIVES

All of the hints thus far in this chapter have been geared to pushing a cart around a supermarket. Here are some other ways to save money:

- **Shop at farmers' markets.** I admit it; I need a 12-step program to help me cure my addiction to local farmers' markets. Shopping alfresco on warm summer days turns picking out fruits and vegetables into a truly sensual experience. Also, you buy only what you want. There are no bunches of carrots; there are individual carrots sold by the pound. The U.S. Deptartment of Agriculture began publishing the *National Directory of Farmers' Markets* in 1994, and at that time the number was fewer than 2,000. That figure has now doubled. To find a farmers' market near you, go to www.ams.usda.gov/farmersmarkets. The first cousins of farmers' markets for small quantities of fruits are the sidewalk vendors in many cities. One great advantage to buying from them is that their fruit is always ripe and ready to eat or cook.

- **Shop at ethnic markets.** If you live in a rural area this may not be possible, but even moderately small cities have a range of ethnic markets, and that's where you should buy ingredients to cook those cuisines. Dried shiitake mushrooms at my local Asian market in Providence are less than 20 percent of the price they are at the supermarket, and the Indian grocery in my neighborhood has ripe mangoes and plantains in addition to exotic spices.

- **Shop alternative stores.** Groceries aren't only at grocery stores; many "dollar stores" and other discount venues stock shelf-stable items. For example, I've been able to find some brands of imported pasta for a fraction of the supermarket cost.

- **Shop online.** In recent years it's become possible to do all your grocery shopping online through such services as Peapod and Fresh Express. While there is frequently a delivery charge involved, for housebound people this is a true boon. If you really hate the thought of pushing the cart, you should explore it; it's impossible to make impulse buys. There are also a large number of online retailers for ethnic foods, dried herbs and spices, premium baking chocolate, and other shelf-stable items. Letting your cursor do the shopping for these items saves you time, and many of them offer free shipping at certain times of year.

So now that you're becoming a grocery guru, you can move on to find myriad ways to save money on your grocery bill while eating wonderfully. That's what *$3 Meals* is all about.

Chapter 2:
Starting with the Basics

Welcome to the most important chapter in this book. You'll be amazed how much further your finite food budget goes after you've learned how easy it is to make at home the high-priced convenience foods from the supermarket aisles. Perhaps you don't think of bottled salad dressings or canned stocks as convenience foods, but that's what they are, and they comprise a slow leak in your weekly budget.

A bottle of salad dressing can be more expensive per ounce than a fine wine, which you'll be able to afford once you stop buying chemical-loaded vinegar and oil to douse your greens. And those bottled marinades are more of an extravagance than eating filet mignon every week; not only are they expensive, but unlike salad dressings, you have to use a large quantity—frequently a whole bottle—to achieve the goal of flavoring food. Then the used marinade must be poured down the sink along with a big hunk of your food budget. In addition to saving money by quickly making these foods, you also can personalize them in myriad ways.

Breadcrumbs? They're an essential part of cooking both for coating foods and as an ingredient to bind foods. Croutons? They're a nice crunchy addition to salads, but ounce for ounce they're much more expensive than the loaves of bread from which they're made. If your house is like mine, you're likely to have stale bread around from time to time, so the cost of making croutons is mere pennies for the utilities to toast the bread, or nothing if you "double team" and bake them when other foods are in the oven.

Another category of essential foods is stock—from a few tablespoons to moisten food to cups and quarts to serve as the base for soups and the gravy for stews. It's the long-simmered homemade stocks that add depth of flavor to the soups and sauces enjoyed at fine restaurants. Classically trained chefs have known for centuries what you're about to learn in this chapter—making stocks is as easy as boiling water and, if you're judicious and save bits and pieces destined for the garbage when prepping foods to be cooked, they're free.

Cans and cartons of stocks are priced in many supermarkets in a confusing way; some prices are calculated by the pound, while others are by the ounce. I looked at a range of costs as well as flavors at a recent taste testing, and found that a generic stock that tasted like salted water with some chemical chicken flavor was a whopping $2 per quart, while ones that actually had some flavor were almost $5 per quart.

While you might not have thought of stocks as a convenience food, surely you knew when using a can of "cream of something soup" to make a casserole that it was a convenience. In fact, has anyone eaten one of those soups diluted? In this chapter you'll learn to make Basic White Sauce that fulfills the same function—without the chemicals.

LIQUID ASSETS

Vinaigrette dressings—the type used most often—are referred to as temporary emulsions; they will stay blended for only a short time and as the dressing is allowed to stand, the oil and vinegar will gradually separate. Traditionally, vinaigrettes were made by laboriously whisking the oil into the vinegar. This makes no sense, because it will separate in a few moments anyway. That's why for these recipes you are instructed to combine all ingredients in a jar with a tight-fitting lid, and shake well.

This is done in two stages, however. The first is to combine the acid—be it any form of vinegar or citrus juice—with the flavorings and seasonings. The reason is that granular substances such as salt or sugar dissolve in water but not in oil, so you want to combine all of those, and then add the oil.

I've often wondered why bottled dressings should be refrigerated after opening; they contain so many preservatives one would think they could survive anything. But your delicious and nutritious homemade dressings should definitely be refrigerated; then allow them to stand at room temperature for 1 hour before serving. Any dressing that contains a dairy product such as sour cream or yogurt, or an egg yolk, should be kept refrigerated at all times until ready to serve.

While many of these recipes were developed for a classic clear vinaigrette, if you want a "creamier" mix, substitute mayonnaise for some or all of the oil. Commercial mayonnaise is made of oil with some other ingredients, and those stabilizers will prevent the dressing from separating as quickly.

STOCKING UP

Think about all those parsley stalks, carrot and onion peelings, and celery leaves that end up in the garbage can after you've cooked dinner.

And now that you are saving money by cutting up your own chickens (see Chapter 5) or breaking down a large chuck roast into stew cubes (see Chapter 6) all of those scraps and bones become valuable assets.

Here's how I navigate the process of stock-making: I keep a few heavy resealable gallon bags in my freezer. Into one go all appropriate vegetable and herb trimmings. Three others are designated for poultry, beef, and fish or seafood trimmings. When one protein bag gets full, I join it with the contents of the vegetable bag, and it's time to make stock.

Once you've made the stock, the next step is to freeze it in a convenient form. Use a measuring tablespoon and calculate the capacity of your ice cube trays. (If you have an automatic ice cube maker, then it's worth the money to buy a plastic tray for this purpose, too.) Freeze some of your stock in the ice cube tray; that's for the times you see "1/4 cup chicken stock" in a recipe. Then freeze the remainder in 1-quart plastic bags. Plastic bags take up less room in the freezer than plastic containers. You can freeze the bags flat on a baking sheet, and then stack them.

Mustard Herb Vinaigrette

This is what most people taste in their mouths when they order a vinaigrette dressing. It is complexly flavored and tart, with some sharp mustard thrown in.

Yield: 1 cup | **Active time:** 10 minutes | **Start to finish:** 10 minutes

2 shallots, peeled and finely chopped
3 garlic cloves, peeled and minced
¼ cup white wine vinegar
2 tablespoons Dijon mustard
1 tablespoon chopped fresh parsley
1 teaspoon dried thyme
1 teaspoon granulated sugar
Salt and freshly ground black pepper to taste
⅔ cup olive oil

Combine shallots, garlic, vinegar, mustard, parsley, thyme, sugar, salt, and pepper in a jar with a tight-fitting lid, and shake well. Add olive oil, and shake well again.

Note: The dressing can be made up to 3 days in advance and refrigerated, tightly covered. Bring it back to room temperature before using.

Balsamic Vinaigrette

In addition to tossed salads, try this as the dressing on cold pasta salads or drizzle it on grilled meat or poultry.

Yield: 1½ cups | **Active time:** 5 minutes | **Start to finish:** 5 minutes

> 2 shallots, peeled and finely chopped
> 3 garlic cloves, peeled and minced
> ⅓ cup balsamic vinegar
> 2 tablespoons Dijon mustard
> 1 tablespoon chopped fresh parsley
> 2 teaspoons herbes de Provence
> Salt and freshly ground black pepper to taste
> ¾ cup extra-virgin olive oil

Combine shallots, garlic, vinegar, mustard, parsley, herbes de Provence, salt, and pepper in a jar with a tight-fitting lid, and shake well. Add olive oil, and shake well again.

Note: The dressing can be made up to 3 days in advance and refrigerated, tightly covered. Bring it back to room temperature before using.

Vinaigrette dressings also make an excellent marinade for meat, poultry, or seafood. Combine equal parts dressing and wine in a heavy resealable plastic bag, and add the food to be marinated. Seafood should be marinated for no more than 30 minutes, while poultry can soak for up to 4 hours, and meats up to 6 hours.

Ginger Vinaigrette

I make a lot of Asian-inspired food, and this salad dressing made with mild rice vinegar complements those dishes well, since it contains characteristic Asian seasoning and sesame oil. This dressing is perfect to transform leftover cold stir-fried vegetables or leftover rice into an exciting dish.

Yield: 1½ cups | **Active time:** 10 minutes | **Start to finish:** 10 minutes

¼ cup sesame seeds*
½ cup rice wine vinegar
¼ cup lime juice
2 tablespoons soy sauce
3 shallots, peeled and minced
3 garlic cloves, peeled and minced
2 tablespoons grated fresh ginger
Salt and freshly ground black pepper to taste
½ cup vegetable oil
¼ cup Asian sesame oil*

1. Place sesame seeds in a small dry skillet over medium heat. Toast seeds, stirring constantly, for 2 minutes, or until lightly brown. Remove the skillet from the heat and set aside.
2. Combine sesame seeds, vinegar, lime juice, soy sauce, shallots, garlic, ginger, salt, and pepper in a jar with a tight-fitting lid, and shake well. Add vegetable oil and sesame oil, and shake well again.

Note: The dressing can be made up to 3 days in advance and refrigerated, tightly covered. Bring it back to room temperature before using.

*Available in the Asian aisle of most supermarkets and in specialty markets.

Greek Feta Dressing

The essence of a Greek salad is a combination of tomatoes, cucumber, and lettuce tossed in a dressing made with sharp feta cheese.

Yield: 1 cup | **Active time:** 10 minutes | **Start to finish:** 10 minutes

¼ cup lemon juice
3 garlic cloves, peeled and minced
2 teaspoons dried oregano
1 teaspoon granulated sugar
Salt and freshly ground black pepper to taste
⅔ cup olive oil
½ cup crumbled feta cheese

Combine lemon juice, garlic, oregano, sugar, salt, and pepper in a jar with a tight-fitting lid, and shake well. Add olive oil, and shake well again. Add feta, and shake gently.

Note: The dressing can be made up to 3 days in advance and refrigerated, tightly covered. Bring it back to room temperature before using.

Honey-Herb Vinaigrette

Cider vinegar is one of the mildest on the market, and also one of the most affordable. A bit of sharp mustard balanced by sweet honey makes this a delicious dressing.

Yield: 1 cup | **Active time:** 10 minutes | **Start to finish:** 10 minutes

- ⅓ cup cider vinegar
- 1 tablespoon Dijon mustard
- 1 tablespoon honey
- 2 tablespoons chopped fresh parsley
- 1 tablespoon herbes de Provence
- 1 shallot, peeled and finely chopped
- 2 garlic cloves, peeled and minced
- Salt and freshly ground black pepper to taste
- ½ cup olive oil

Combine vinegar, mustard, honey, parsley, herbes de Provence, shallot, garlic, salt, and pepper in a jar with a tight-fitting lid, and shake well. Add olive oil, and shake well again.

Note: The dressing can be made up to 3 days in advance and refrigerated, tightly covered. Bring it back to room temperature before using.

Blue Cheese Dressing

Blue cheese is not only a classic dressing for salads; it can also be served at parties as a dip for vegetable crudité. If you're going to be serving all the dressing at once, reserve some of the cheese to sprinkle over the food rather than including all of it in the dressing.

Yield: 1½ cups | **Active time:** 5 minutes | **Start to finish:** 5 minutes

> ¾ cup mayonnaise
> ½ cup sour cream
> 2 tablespoons white wine vinegar
> ⅓ pound blue cheese, crumbled
> Salt and freshly ground black pepper to taste

Combine mayonnaise, sour cream, and vinegar in a mixing bowl, and whisk until smooth. Stir in the blue cheese, and season to taste with salt and pepper. Refrigerate until well chilled.

Note: The dressing can be made up to 3 days in advance and refrigerated, tightly covered.

Thousand Island Dressing (aka Russian Dressing)

There is basically no difference between Thousand Island dressing and Russian dressing; the two names are used in different parts of the country for the same mix of mayonnaise with chili sauce and other seasonings. It's popular for salads, and essential for such treats as a Reuben sandwich.

Yield: 1½ cups | **Active time:** 10 minutes | **Start to finish:** 10 minutes

1 cup mayonnaise

⅓ cup bottled chili sauce

2 tablespoons lemon juice

¼ cup chopped drained pimiento

2 scallions, white parts and 3 inches of green tops, rinsed, trimmed, and chopped

2 tablespoons sweet pickle relish

2 tablespoons Dijon mustard

Salt and freshly ground black pepper to taste

Combine mayonnaise, chili sauce, lemon juice, pimiento, scallions, pickle relish, mustard, salt, and pepper in a mixing bowl. Whisk well. Refrigerate until well chilled.

Note: The dressing can be made up to 3 days in advance and refrigerated, tightly covered.

Variations: Here are some ideas for personalizing this dressing:

- Some recipes call for 1 finely chopped hard-cooked egg; that creates a thicker dressing.
- You can also add 2 tablespoons of chopped fresh parsley or dill to add a green color and the flavor of the herb.

Classic Caesar Dressing

Caesar salad has nothing to do with Rome. It was the invention of Caesar Cardini, who owned a restaurant in Tijuana, Mexico. This dressing, laced with garlic and anchovy paste, is close to the original. To turn this salad into a full meal, top it with slices of some type of meat or seafood you may have left over from another meal.

Yield: 1½ cups | **Active time:** 10 minutes | **Start to finish:** 15 minutes

    1 large egg
    1 (2-ounce) tube anchovy paste
    5 garlic cloves, peeled and minced
    ¼ cup lemon juice
    2 tablespoons Dijon mustard
    ½ cup olive oil
    ½ cup freshly grated Parmesan cheese
    Freshly ground black pepper to taste

1. Bring a small saucepan of water to a boil over high heat. Add egg and boil for 1 minute. Remove egg from the water with a slotted spoon, and break it into a jar with a tight-fitting lid, scraping the inside of the shell.

2. Add anchovy paste, garlic, lemon juice, and mustard, and shake well. Add olive oil and Parmesan, and season to taste with pepper. Shake well again. Refrigerate until well chilled.

Note: The dressing can be made up to 3 days in advance and refrigerated, tightly covered.

Spicy Citrus Marinade

Here's a good all-purpose marinade for poultry, pork, and seafood. It has a good balance of sweet and hot, and penetrates food quickly.

Yield: 1½ cups | **Active time:** 10 minutes | **Start to finish:** 10 minutes

³/₄ cup orange juice
3 tablespoons lime juice
2 tablespoons soy sauce
2 teaspoons crumbled dried rosemary
3 garlic cloves, peeled and minced
2 tablespoons chili powder
Freshly ground black pepper to taste
¹/₄ cup olive oil

Combine orange juice, lime juice, soy sauce, rosemary, garlic, chili powder, and pepper in a heavy resealable plastic bag, and mix well. Add oil, and mix well again. Add food to be marinated, turning the bag to coat food evenly.

Note: The marinade can be refrigerated for up to 3 days.

Variations: The basis of this marinade is the combination of citrus juices, but here are some other ways to prepare it:

- Omit the chili powder, and substitute 2 tablespoons smoked Spanish paprika.

- Substitute white wine for the orange juice, and add 1 tablespoon granulated sugar.

Fruits such as papaya and pineapple contain natural meat tenderizers in their skins. If using one of these fruits, save the skins and add them to the marinade. They won't add much, if any, flavor, but they will tenderize foods even faster.

Red Wine Marinade

Less expensive cuts of beef, such as round steaks, London broil, and skirt steaks, can be tenderized as well as flavored by marinating in this combination of acids for up to 8 hours, and then being grilled or broiled.

Yield: 1½ cups | **Active time:** 10 minutes | **Start to finish:** 10 minutes

⅔ cup dry red wine
2 tablespoons balsamic vinegar
2 tablespoons firmly packed dark brown sugar
2 tablespoons chopped fresh parsley
1 tablespoon dried thyme
3 large garlic cloves, peeled and minced
2 bay leaves, broken in half
Salt and freshly ground black pepper to taste
¼ cup olive oil

Combine wine, vinegar, brown sugar, parsley, thyme, garlic, bay leaves, salt, and pepper in a heavy resealable plastic bag, and mix well. Add oil, and mix well again. Add food to be marinated, turning the bag to coat food evenly.

Note: The marinade can be refrigerated for up to 3 days.

I have a great use for the leftover red wine; I drink it. But to preserve most of a bottle for future cooking, here's what to do: Boil it down in a saucepan until it's reduced by half, then freeze it in ice cube trays. When you're making a sauce in the future that calls for red wine, just pull out a few cubes.

Cocktail Sauce

Ah, the condiment aisle of the supermarket is loaded with high-priced items with limited use, and cocktail sauce fits into that category. While it's certainly necessary when eating a seafood cocktail, you'll eat the seafood cocktail more often if you save money on the sauce.

Yield: 1 cup | **Active time:** 10 minutes | **Start to finish:** 10 minutes

> ³/₄ cup bottled chili sauce
> 3 tablespoons prepared white horseradish
> 3 tablespoons lemon juice
> 1 tablespoon Worcestershire sauce
> 1 tablespoon soy sauce
> ½ teaspoon hot red pepper sauce, or to taste

Combine chili sauce, horseradish, lemon juice, Worcestershire sauce, soy sauce, and hot red pepper sauce in a mixing bowl. Whisk well. Scrape mixture into an airtight container, and refrigerate until serving.

Note: The sauce can be made up to 5 days in advance and refrigerated, tightly covered.

Variations: Here are some ideas for personalizing cocktail sauce:
- Rather than adding hot pepper sauce, add 1 or 2 finely chopped chipotle chiles in adobo sauce for a smoky, Mexican flavor.
- For a milder sauce, use ketchup instead of chili sauce and cut back on the amount of horseradish.

Basic Barbecue Sauce

When you look at the component ingredients of a commercial barbecue sauce, none of them is as expensive as the sauce itself, and many sauces are loaded with chemicals. This is a sauce I developed many years ago, and swear by it for all my cooking. Even with the inclusion of a fresh lemon and some ginger, it's still a fraction of the price of bottled sauce—and it's delicious.

Yield: 4 cups | **Active time:** 10 minutes | **Start to finish:** 40 minutes

1 (20-ounce) bottle ketchup
1 cup cider vinegar
½ cup firmly packed dark brown sugar
5 tablespoons Worcestershire sauce
¼ cup vegetable oil
2 tablespoons dry mustard powder
2 garlic cloves, peeled and minced
1 tablespoon grated fresh ginger
1 lemon, thinly sliced
½ to 1 teaspoon hot red pepper sauce, or to taste

1. Combine ketchup, vinegar, brown sugar, Worcestershire sauce, vegetable oil, mustard, garlic, ginger, lemon, and red pepper sauce in a heavy 2-quart saucepan, and bring to a boil over medium heat, stirring occasionally.
2. Reduce the heat to low and simmer sauce, uncovered, for 30 minutes, or until thick, stirring occasionally. Strain sauce, pressing with the back of a spoon to extract as much liquid as possible. Ladle the sauce into containers and refrigerate, tightly covered.

Note: The sauce can be made up to 1 week in advance and refrigerated, tightly covered. Bring it back to room temperature before serving. It can also be frozen for up to 3 months.

Herbed Tomato Sauce

This easy-to-make sauce takes the place of purchased marinara sauce in your repertoire, and because it freezes so well you can keep a batch around at all times.

Yield: 2½ cups | **Active time:** 15 minutes | **Start to finish:** 1 hour

> ¼ cup olive oil
> 1 medium onion, peeled and finely chopped
> 4 garlic cloves, peeled and minced
> 1 carrot, peeled and finely chopped
> 1 celery rib, rinsed, trimmed, and finely chopped
> 1 (28-ounce) can crushed tomatoes
> 2 tablespoons chopped fresh parsley
> 2 teaspoons dried oregano
> 1 teaspoon dried thyme
> 2 bay leaves
> Salt and freshly ground black pepper to taste

1. Heat olive oil in 2-quart saucepan over medium heat. Add onion and garlic and cook, stirring frequently, for 3 minutes, or until onion is translucent.
2. Add carrot, celery, tomatoes, parsley, oregano, thyme, and bay leaves. Bring to a boil, reduce the heat to low, and simmer sauce, uncovered, stirring occasionally, for 40 minutes, or until lightly thickened. Season to taste with salt and pepper.

Note: The sauce can be made up to 3 days in advance and refrigerated, tightly covered. Bring back to a simmer before serving. It can also be frozen for up to 3 months.

Easy Aioli

Aioli, which is just a garlicky mayonnaise, is the ketchup of Provençal French cooking, and it's now available in many upscale supermarkets at ridiculously high prices. Here's how to make it easily and inexpensively.

Yield: 2 cups | **Active time:** 10 minutes | **Start to finish:** 10 minutes

> 1½ cups mayonnaise
> 6 garlic cloves, peeled and pushed through a garlic press
> 3 tablespoons lemon juice
> 2 tablespoons Dijon mustard
> Salt and freshly ground black pepper to taste

Combine mayonnaise, garlic, lemon juice, and mustard in a mixing bowl. Whisk well, and season to taste with salt and pepper. Refrigerate until ready to use.

Note: The sauce can be made up to 3 days in advance and refrigerated, tightly covered. Bring it back to room temperature before serving.

Variations: A lot of ingredients go well with mayonnaise and garlic, so try these:

- Add 2 tablespoons chili powder.
- Add ¼ cup pureed roasted red bell pepper.

Tartar Sauce

Tartar sauce is the traditional accompaniment to fried fish and seafood, and it has a mayonnaise base, so the primary ingredient is ready and handy.

Yield: 2 cups | **Active time:** 10 minutes | **Start to finish:** 10 minutes

1½ cups mayonnaise
¼ cup finely chopped sweet pickle
2 scallions, white parts and 2 inches of green tops, rinsed, trimmed, and chopped
3 tablespoons small capers, drained, rinsed, and chopped
2 tablespoons white wine vinegar
2 tablespoons chopped fresh parsley
1 teaspoon dried tarragon
Salt and freshly ground black pepper to taste

Combine mayonnaise, pickle, scallions, capers, vinegar, parsley, and tarragon in a mixing bowl. Whisk well, and season to taste with salt and pepper. Refrigerate until ready to use.

Note: The sauce can be made up to 3 days in advance and refrigerated, tightly covered. Bring it back to room temperature before serving.

Spicy Thai Peanut Sauce

This sauce is the "utility infielder" of Asian sauces, which is why it is now found bottled at a high price with other Asian condiments. It can be used as a dipping sauce for grilled chicken or pork chops, or tossed with leftover pasta and vegetables for a delicious cold salad.

Yield: 2 cups | **Active time:** 10 minutes | **Start to finish:** 30 minutes, including 20 minutes for chilling

1 cup chunky peanut butter
½ cup very hot tap water
½ cup firmly packed dark brown sugar
⅓ cup lime juice
¼ cup soy sauce
2 tablespoons Asian sesame oil*
2 tablespoons Chinese chile paste with garlic*
6 garlic cloves, peeled and minced
3 scallions, white parts and 3 inches of green tops, rinsed, trimmed and chopped
¼ cup chopped fresh cilantro

Combine peanut butter, water, brown sugar, lime juice, soy sauce, sesame oil, and chile paste in a mixing bowl. Whisk until well combined. Stir in garlic, scallions, and cilantro, and chill well before serving.

Note: The sauce can be made up to 5 days in advance and refrigerated, tightly covered. Bring it back to room temperature before serving.

* Available in the Asian aisle of most supermarkets and in specialty markets.

> To save time when making a recipe with many liquid ingredients, measure them into the same large cup, calculating what the level should be after each addition.

Sweet and Sour Sauce

Here's another Asian sauce you'll never spend money to buy again, and it's far more delicious than any of those overly thickened sauces you buy which are usually in a color rarely found in nature.

Yield: 1½ cups | **Active time:** 15 minutes | **Start to finish:** 20 minutes

> 2 tablespoons vegetable oil
> 4 scallions, white parts and 2 inches of green tops, rinsed, trimmed, and chopped
> 2 garlic cloves, peeled and minced
> 2 tablespoons grated fresh ginger
> ½ cup finely chopped pineapple
> ½ cup rice vinegar
> ⅓ cup ketchup
> ¼ cup firmly packed dark brown sugar
> 2 tablespoons Chinese chile paste with garlic*
> 1 tablespoon soy sauce
> 1 tablespoon cornstarch
> 1 tablespoon cold water

1. Heat oil in a small saucepan over medium-high heat. Add scallions, garlic, and ginger, and cook, stirring frequently, for 3 minutes, or until scallions are translucent.
2. Add pineapple, vinegar, ketchup, sugar, chile paste, and soy sauce to the pan, and stir. Bring to a boil over medium-high heat, stirring occasionally. Reduce heat to low, and simmer, uncovered, for 5 minutes.
3. Combine cornstarch and water in a small cup, and stir well. Add mixture to the pan, and cook for 1 minute, or until slightly thickened. Serve sauce at room temperature or chilled.

Note: The sauce can be refrigerated for up to 1 week.

Variations: Here are some alterations you can make to this recipe:
- Substitute mango or papaya for the pineapple.
- Omit the chile paste if you want a sauce with no "heat."

* Available in the Asian aisle of most supermarkets and in specialty markets.

> Be careful with the salt shaker. Soy sauce is very high in sodium and performs the same function as salt in cooking.

Basic White Sauce

White sauces form the base for a range of dishes from creamed soups to macaroni and cheese and Italian lasagna. They are made with either milk or stock, and thickened with a roux made from cooking butter with flour.

Yield: 2 cups | **Active time:** 15 minutes | **Start to finish:** 20 minutes

> 3 tablespoons unsalted butter
> 3 tablespoons all-purpose flour
> 2 cups hot whole milk
> Salt and freshly ground black pepper to taste

1. Melt butter in a saucepan over low heat. Stir in flour, and cook, stirring constantly, for 2 minutes, or until mixture bubbles.
2. Slowly but steadily pour milk into the pan, whisking constantly, over medium heat until sauce comes to a boil. Simmer 2–3 minutes, thinning with more liquid if necessary to reach the right consistency. Season to taste with salt and pepper.

Note: The sauce can be made up to 3 days in advance and refrigerated, tightly covered. Reheat it over low heat, stirring occasionally, or in a microwave oven.

Variations: Here are some additions and substitutions you can make to this basic sauce:

- Add ³⁄₄ cup grated cheese (cheddar, smoked cheddar, Swiss, Gruyère) to the thickened sauce, and cook over low heat until the cheese melts.
- Add 2–3 tablespoons smooth or grainy Dijon mustard.
- Substitute ½ cup dry white wine for ½ cup of the milk, and add 3–4 tablespoons chopped fresh herbs.
- Substitute 1 cup chicken stock for 1 cup of milk; this will produce a lighter sauce.

> If the sauce is lumpy, push it through a sieve, and then whisk it again to a simmer over low heat. Also, all white sauces form a skin as they cool. Push a sheet of plastic wrap directly into the surface of the sauce or whisk it as it cools to prevent this from happening.

Basic Breadcrumbs

Making breadcrumbs at home is an easy way to pare down the grocery bill, especially if you are making bread yourself; there are many options in Chapter 8.

Yield: 2 cups | **Active time:** 10 minutes | **Start to finish:** 2 hours

¼ pound sliced white bread, preferably stale

1. Preheat the oven to 200°F, and line a baking sheet with aluminum foil.
2. Spread bread out in a single layer on the baking sheet, and bake for 1½–1¾ hours, or until totally dry. Remove the pan from the oven, and allow bread to cool.
3. Break bread into 1-inch cubes, and grind in a food processor fitted with the steel blade. Store breadcrumbs in an airtight container.

Note: The breadcrumbs will keep for up to 3 months.

Variations: Once you have the basic breadcrumbs in the house, it's easy to modify them:

- This recipe creates what are called fresh breadcrumbs. For toasted breadcrumbs, bake the bread in a 375°F oven for 10–12 minutes per side, turning slices with a spatula, or until browned.
- Italian breadcrumbs are toasted breadcrumbs seasoned with parsley, other herbs, garlic, and Parmesan cheese. To create them at home, add 1 teaspoon Italian seasoning, ½ teaspoon garlic powder, and 3 tablespoons Parmesan cheese to each 1 cup plain breadcrumbs.

Basic Croutons

Crunchy bits of toast on top of a salad add textural variety, and for some recipes, such as Caesar Salad, they are specified. They are also a snap to make with stale bread. While some recipes call for sautéing them on top of the stove, I find it is much easier to bake them.

Yield: 3 cups | **Active time:** 10 minutes | **Start to finish:** 20 minutes

> 3 cups (½-inch) cubes French or Italian bread
> ⅓ cup olive oil
> Salt and freshly ground black pepper to taste

1. Preheat the oven to 375°F, and line a baking pan with aluminum foil.
2. Place bread cubes in the baking pan, drizzle bread with olive oil, and sprinkle with salt and pepper. Toss cubes to coat evenly.
3. Bake cubes for a total of 10 minutes, or until brown and crunchy, turning them with a spatula after 5 minutes. Remove the pan from the oven, and allow cubes to reach room temperature. Store in an airtight container or resealable plastic bag at room temperature.

Note: The croutons can be prepared up to 1 week in advance and kept at room temperature in an airtight container.

Variations: Here are some ways to jazz up this recipe:

- Press 2 garlic cloves through a garlic press, and stir the garlic into the oil.
- Rather than using French bread, substitute herb bread, olive bread, or multi-grain bread.
- Toss croutons with 1 tablespoon Italian seasoning or herbes de Provence before baking.
- Toss croutons with 3 tablespoons freshly grated Parmesan cheese before baking.

Chicken Stock

Richly flavored, homemade chicken stock is as important as good olive oil in my kitchen. Once you've gotten into the habit of "keeping stocked," you'll appreciate the difference that it makes in all soups and sauces. And making it is as easy as boiling water.

Yield: 4 quarts | **Active time:** 10 minutes | **Start to finish:** 4 hours

> 6 quarts water
> 5 pounds chicken bones, skin, and trimmings
> 4 celery ribs, rinsed and cut into thick slices
> 2 onions, trimmed and quartered
> 2 carrots, trimmed, scrubbed, and cut into thick slices
> 2 tablespoons whole black peppercorns
> 6 garlic cloves, peeled
> 4 sprigs parsley
> 1 teaspoon dried thyme
> 2 bay leaves

1. Place water and chicken in a large stockpot, and bring to a boil over high heat. Reduce the heat to low, and skim off foam that rises during the first 10–15 minutes of simmering. Simmer stock, uncovered, for 1 hour, then add celery, onions, carrots, peppercorns, garlic, parsley, thyme, and bay leaves. Simmer for 2½ hours.

2. Strain stock through a fine-meshed sieve, pushing with the back of a spoon to extract as much liquid as possible. Discard solids, spoon stock into smaller containers, and refrigerate. Remove and discard fat from surface of stock, then transfer stock to a variety of container sizes.

Note: The stock can be refrigerated and used within 3 days, or it can be frozen for up to 6 months.

Variation: Want to make a dish with turkey? Try this:
- Use the same amount of turkey giblets and necks as chicken pieces.

Beef Stock

While beef stock is not specified as often as chicken stock in recipes, it is the backbone to certain soups and the gravy for stews and roasts.

Yield: 2 quarts | **Active time:** 15 minutes | **Start to finish:** 3½ hours

> 2 pounds beef trimmings (bones and fat) or inexpensive beef shank
> 3 quarts water
> 1 carrot, trimmed, scrubbed, and cut into thick slices
> 1 medium onion, peeled and sliced
> 1 celery rib, trimmed and sliced
> 1 tablespoon whole black peppercorns
> 3 sprigs fresh parsley
> 1 teaspoon dried thyme
> 2 garlic cloves, peeled
> 2 bay leaves

1. Preheat the oven broiler, and line a broiler pan with heavy duty aluminum foil. Broil beef for 3 minutes per side, or until browned. Transfer beef to a large stockpot, and add water. Bring to a boil over high heat. Reduce the heat to low, and skim off foam that rises during the first 10–15 minutes of simmering. Simmer for 1 hour, uncovered, then add carrot, onion, celery, peppercorns, parsley, thyme, garlic, and bay leaves. Simmer for 3 hours.

2. Strain stock through a fine-meshed sieve, pushing with the back of a spoon to extract as much liquid as possible. Discard solids, and spoon stock into smaller containers. Refrigerate. Remove and discard fat from surface of stock.

Note: The stock can be refrigerated and used within 3 days, or it can be frozen for up to 6 months.

Vegetable Stock

You may think it not necessary to use vegetable stock if making a vegetarian dish that includes the same vegetables, but that's not the case. Using stock creates a much more richly flavored dish that can't be replicated by increasing the quantity of vegetables cooked in it.

Yield: 2 quarts | **Active time:** 10 minutes | **Start to finish:** 1 hour

2 quarts water

2 carrots, scrubbed, trimmed, and thinly sliced

2 celery ribs, trimmed and sliced

2 leeks, white part only, trimmed, rinsed, and thinly sliced

1 small onion, peeled and thinly sliced

1 tablespoon whole black peppercorns

3 sprigs fresh parsley

1 teaspoon dried thyme

2 garlic cloves, peeled

1 bay leaf

1. Pour water into a stock pot, and add carrots, celery, leeks, onion, peppercorns, parsley, thyme, garlic, and bay leaf. Bring to a boil over high heat, then reduce the heat to low and simmer stock, uncovered, for 1 hour.

2. Strain stock through a fine-meshed sieve, pushing with the back of a spoon to extract as much liquid as possible. Discard solids, and allow stock to cool to room temperature. Spoon stock into smaller containers, and refrigerate.

Note: The stock can be refrigerated and used within 3 days, or it can be frozen for up to 6 months.

Seafood Stock

Seafood stock is a great reason to make friends with head of the fish department of your supermarket, or a fishmonger, if you're lucky enough to live near a store devoted to fish and seafood. You can arrange in advance to have them save the lobster bodies for you if the store cooks lobster meat, or purchase them at minimal cost. You can also ask for free or inexpensive fish bones, if the store actually fillets the fish on site.

Yield: 2 quarts | **Active time:** 15 minutes | **Start to finish:** 1³/₄ hours

> 3 lobster bodies (whole lobsters from which the tail and claw meat has been removed), shells from 3 pounds raw shrimp, or 2 pounds bones and skin from firm-fleshed white fish such as halibut, cod, or sole
> 3 quarts water
> 1 cup dry white wine
> 1 carrot, scrubbed, trimmed, and cut into 1-inch chunks
> 1 medium onion, peeled and sliced
> 1 celery rib, rinsed, trimmed, and sliced
> 1 tablespoon whole black peppercorns
> 3 sprigs fresh parsley
> 1 teaspoon dried thyme
> 2 garlic cloves, peeled
> 1 bay leaf

1. If using lobster shells, pull top shell off 1 lobster body. Scrape off and discard feathery gills, then break body into small pieces. Place pieces into the stockpot, and repeat with remaining lobster bodies. If using shrimp shells or fish bones, rinse and place in the stockpot.
2. Add water, wine, carrot, onion, celery, peppercorns, parsley, thyme, garlic, and bay leaf. Bring to a boil over high heat, then reduce the heat to low and simmer stock, uncovered, for 1¹/₂ hours.

3. Strain stock through a fine-meshed sieve, pushing with the back of a spoon to extract as much liquid as possible. Discard solids, and allow stock to cool to room temperature. Spoon stock into smaller containers, and refrigerate.

Note: The stock can be refrigerated and used within 3 days, or it can be frozen for up to 6 months.

Variations: As with all stock recipes, you can make endless changes and still achieve a good result:

- Instead of white wine, you can substitute ¾ cup white vermouth for the same flavor.
- Substitute tarragon for the thyme for a lighter flavor.

Seafood stock is perhaps the hardest to make if you don't live near the coast. A good substitute is bottled clam juice. Use it in place of the water, and simmer it with vegetables and wine to intensify its flavor.

Chapter 3:
Meals in a Bowl

In Alice in Wonderland, Lewis Carroll writes "Beautiful soup! Who cares for fish, game, or any other dish? Who would not give all else for two pennyworth only of beautiful soup?" I couldn't agree with him more. A steaming bowl of soup fills the soul as well as the stomach; a bowl of soup provides emotional reassurance as well as healthy ingredients.

While thin soups like consommé can be emotionally fulfilling, those aren't the recipes you'll find in this chapter. Herein are soups that don't *start* a meal; they *are* the meal. They are thick and hearty, and filled with many healthful ingredients.

If they're made with good homemade stocks, the recipes for which you'll find in Chapter 2, they are also extremely inexpensive to make. With homemade stocks, these tummy-filling soups are less than $2 per serving to make, and with a bread from Chapter 8 and a tossed salad, your meal is complete.

Cuban Black Bean Soup

Garlic and aromatic spices like cumin and coriander add sparkle to this thick and hearty vegetarian soup. Add a tossed salad and some garlic bread, and the meal is complete.

Yield: 4–6 servings | **Active time:** 15 minutes | **Start to finish:** 2 hours, including 1 hour for soaking beans

1 pound dried black beans
¼ cup olive oil
1 large onion, peeled and diced
1 green bell pepper, seeds and ribs removed, and finely chopped
6 garlic cloves, peeled and minced
1–2 jalapeño or serrano chiles, seeds and ribs removed, and finely chopped
2 tablespoons ground cumin

1 tablespoon ground coriander
6 cups Vegetable Stock (recipe on page 35) or purchased stock
¼ cup chopped fresh cilantro
Salt and freshly ground black pepper to taste
Sour cream (optional)
Lime wedges (optional)

1. Soak beans in cold water to cover for a minimum of 6 hours, or preferably overnight. Or, place beans in a saucepan covered with water, and bring to a boil over high heat. Boil for 1 minute, turn off the heat, and cover the pan. Allow beans to soak for 1 hour, then drain. With either method, continue with the dish as soon as beans have soaked, or refrigerate beans.

2. Heat oil in a 3-quart saucepan over medium-high heat. Add onion, green bell pepper, garlic, and chiles. Cook, stirring frequently, for 3 minutes, or until onion is translucent. Reduce the heat to low, and stir in cumin and coriander. Cook, stirring constantly, for 1 minute.

3. Add beans and stock, and bring to a boil over high heat, stirring occasionally. Reduce the heat to low, and simmer soup, partially covered, for 1–1¼ hours, or until beans are soft.

4. Remove 2 cups of beans with a slotted spoon, and puree in a food processor fitted with a steel blade or in a blender. Return beans to the soup, stir in cilantro, season to taste with salt and pepper, and serve hot. Top with a dollop of sour cream and serve with lime wedges, if using.

Note: The soup can be made up to 2 days in advance and refrigerated, tightly covered. Reheat it over low heat, covered.

There's no question that chiles contain potent oils; however, there's no need to wear rubber gloves when handling them. I cut the chiles on a glass plate rather than on my cutting board so the volatile oils do not penetrate it. What's most important is that you wash your hands thoroughly after handling chiles.

Sweet and Sour Red Cabbage Soup

Red cabbage is the mild cousin in the family, and its inherent sweetness is amplified by hints of heady balsamic vinegar contrasted with brown sugar. Red cabbage also contains many antioxidant vitamins, making this a healthy as well as hearty soup.

Yield: 4–6 servings | **Active time:** 20 minutes | **Start to finish:** 1¼ hours

 1 (1½-pound) head red cabbage
 2 tablespoons vegetable oil
 1 large red onion, peeled and diced
 2 garlic cloves, peeled and minced
 5 cups Vegetable Stock (recipe on page 35) or purchased stock
 1 (14.5-ounce) can crushed tomatoes, undrained
 ¼ cup balsamic vinegar
 ¼ cup firmly packed dark brown sugar
 2 tablespoons chopped fresh parsley
 1 teaspoon dried thyme
 1 bay leaf
 Salt and freshly ground black pepper to taste
 4–6 tablespoons sour cream (optional)

1. Discard outer leaves from red cabbage. Cut cabbage in half and discard core. Shred cabbage finely, and set aside; this can be done quickly using a food processor fitted with a thin slicing disc.
2. Heat oil in a 3-quart saucepan over medium-high heat. Add onion and garlic, and cook, stirring frequently, for 3 minutes, or until onion is translucent. Add cabbage, stock, tomatoes, balsamic vinegar, brown sugar, parsley, thyme, and bay leaf. Bring to a boil over high heat, stirring occasionally.
3. Reduce the heat to low, and simmer soup, partially covered, for 1 hour, or until cabbage is very tender. Remove and discard bay leaf, season to taste with salt and pepper, and serve hot, garnished with sour cream, if using.

Note: The soup can be made up to 2 days in advance and refrigerated, tightly covered. Reheat it over low heat, covered.

Caribbean Curried Seafood Soup

While curry is most often associated with Indian cooking, it's also a flavor at home in the West Indies because of the traffic during the colonial spice trade. This soup appears creamy from coconut milk, which also softens the heat from chiles.

Yield: 4–6 servings | **Active time:** 15 minutes | **Start to finish:** 35 minutes

     2 tablespoons olive oil
     2 medium onions, peeled and diced
     1 celery rib, rinsed, trimmed, and diced
     4 garlic cloves, peeled and minced
     1 jalapeño or serrano chile, seeds and ribs removed, and finely chopped
     2 tablespoons curry powder
     1 (14.5-ounce) can diced tomatoes, undrained
     3 cups canned light coconut milk
     1 (8-ounce) bottle clam juice
     1 (15-ounce) can black beans, drained and rinsed
     1 (10-ounce) package frozen peas, thawed
     1 pound fish fillets, rinsed and cut into $3/4$-inch cubes
     Salt and freshly ground black pepper to taste
     3–4 cups cooked white or brown rice, hot

1. Heat oil in 3-quart saucepan over medium-high heat. Add onions, celery, garlic, and chile, and cook, stirring frequently, for 3 minutes, or until onions are translucent. Reduce the heat to low, add curry powder, and cook for 1 minute, stirring constantly. Add tomatoes, coconut milk, and clam juice. Bring to a boil over medium heat, stirring occasionally.

2. Cover the pan, reduce the heat to low, and cook for 15 minutes. Add black beans, peas, and fish, and cook, covered, over low heat for 3–5 minutes, or until fish is opaque and cooked through. Season to taste with salt and pepper, and serve immediately over rice.

Note: The soup can be prepared up to 1 day in advance and refrigerated, tightly covered. Reheat it, covered, over low heat, stirring occasionally.

Variation: Not in the mood for fish? Try this:
- Substitute 1 pound boneless, skinless chicken meat, cut into $1/2$-inch cubes. Add the chicken at the same time as the tomatoes and coconut milk. Also, substitute 1 cup chicken stock for the clam juice.

Seafood Gumbo

Gumbo is a classic dish from the Louisiana bayous; the name comes from the African word for okra, which is used as the thickening agent. This version is only mildly spicy, but feel free to add more hot red pepper sauce if you like fiery flavors.

Yield: 6–8 servings | **Active time:** 15 minutes | **Start to finish:** 1 hour

½ cup vegetable oil
¾ cup all-purpose flour
2 tablespoons unsalted butter
1 large onion, peeled and diced
1 large green bell pepper, seeds and ribs removed, and diced
2 celery ribs, rinsed, trimmed, and diced
5 garlic cloves, peeled and minced
4 cups Seafood Stock (recipe on page 36) or bottled clam juice
1 teaspoon dried thyme
2 bay leaves
1 (14.5-ounce) can diced tomatoes, undrained
½ teaspoon hot red pepper sauce, or to taste
1 (1-pound) bag frozen sliced okra, thawed
1½ pounds fish fillets, rinsed and cut into ¾-inch cubes
3 tablespoons chopped fresh parsley
Salt and freshly ground black pepper to taste
3–4 cups cooked white or brown rice, hot

1. Preheat the oven to 450°F. Combine oil and flour in a Dutch oven, and place the pan in the oven. Bake roux for 20–30 minutes, or until walnut brown, stirring occasionally.
2. While roux bakes, heat butter in large skillet over medium-high heat. Add onion, green pepper, celery, and garlic. Cook, stirring frequently, for 3 minutes, or until onion is translucent. Set aside.
3. Remove roux from oven, and place the pan on the stove over medium heat. Add stock and whisk constantly, until mixture comes to a boil and thickens. Add vegetable mixture, thyme, bay leaves, tomatoes, and red pepper sauce to the pan. Bring to a boil, cover, and cook over low heat for 20 minutes, stirring occasionally. Add okra, and cook for an additional 10 minutes, or until okra is very tender.

4. Add fish and parsley. Bring back to a boil and cook, covered, over low heat for 3–5 minutes, or until fish is opaque and cooked through. Remove and discard bay leaves, season to taste with salt and pepper, and serve immediately over rice.

Note: The soup can be prepared up to 2 days in advance and refrigerated, tightly covered. Reheat it, covered, over low heat, stirring frequently.

Variations: The name "gumbo" refers to the okra and roux, and there are many other ingredients to add:

- Replace ½ pound seafood with andouille or another smoked sausage. Brown sausage with the vegetables, and add it to the gumbo along with the stock.
- Transform this recipe into Chicken Gumbo by substituting 1½ pounds boneless, skinless chicken meat for the fish, and chicken stock for the seafood stock.

Roux, pronounced *ROO*, as in kangaroo, is a mixture of fat and flour used as a thickening agent for soups and sauces. The first step in all roux is to cook the flour, so that the dish doesn't taste like library paste. For white sauces, this is done over low heat and the fat used is butter. Many Creole and Cajun dishes, such as gumbo, use a fuller-flavored brown roux made with oil or drippings and cooked until a deep brown. The dark roux gives dishes an almost nutty flavor.

New England Clam Chowder

Early chowder recipes call for everything from beer to ketchup, but not milk. What we know as New England chowder dates from the mid-nineteenth century. My version includes celery and herbs, which create a more complex flavor.

Yield: 4–6 servings | **Active time:** 20 minutes | **Start to finish:** 40 minutes

> 1 pint fresh minced clams
> 4 tablespoons (½ stick) unsalted butter, divided
> 2 medium onions, peeled and diced
> 2 celery ribs, rinsed, trimmed, and diced
> 1 (8-ounce) bottle clam juice
> 2 medium redskin potatoes, scrubbed and cut into ½-inch dice
> 2 tablespoons chopped fresh parsley
> 1 bay leaf
> 1 teaspoon dried thyme
> Salt and freshly ground black pepper to taste
> 3 tablespoons all-purpose flour
> 3 cups whole milk

1. Drain clams in a sieve over a bowl, reserving the juice in the bowl. Press down with the back of a spoon to extract as much liquid as possible from clams.
2. Melt 2 tablespoons butter in a 2-quart saucepan over medium heat. Add onions and celery, and cook, stirring frequently, for 3 minutes, or until onions are translucent. Add bottled clam juice and reserved clam juice to the pan, along with potatoes, parsley, bay leaf, thyme, salt, and pepper. Bring to a boil, reduce the heat to low, and simmer, covered, for 10–12 minutes, or until potatoes are tender.
3. While mixture simmers, melt remaining butter in a small saucepan over low heat. Stir in flour and cook, stirring constantly, for 2 minutes. Raise the heat to medium and whisk in milk. Bring to a boil, whisking frequently, and simmer for 2 minutes.
4. Stir thickened milk into the pot with the vegetables, and add clams. Bring to a boil, reduce the heat to low, and simmer, uncovered, for 3 minutes. Remove and discard bay leaf, season to taste with salt and pepper, and serve hot.

Note: The soup can be made up to 2 days in advance and refrigerated, tightly covered. Reheat over low heat, stirring occasionally, and do not allow it to boil or the clams will toughen.

Variations: There are lots of ways to glamorize this classic:
- Start by cooking $\frac{1}{4}$ pound bacon until crisp, and then use 2 tablespoons bacon fat instead of butter to sauté the vegetables. Crumble the bacon and add it to the soup along with the clams.
- Add 1 cup cooked corn kernels along with the clams.
- Cook $\frac{1}{2}$ green bell pepper, finely chopped, along with the onions.

There are times that friendly fishmongers will give you leftover clam juice from a vat of minced clams. That's a great treat, and it saves money. But always strain the juice through a sieve lined with a paper coffee filter or a paper towel to ensure that there are no shell fragments or sand in it.

Manhattan Clam Chowder

This tomato-based fish soup is extremely low in calories, while it's very high in flavor. Serve a tossed salad with it, and one of the breads in Chapter 8.

Yield: 4–6 servings | **Active time:** 30 minutes | **Start to finish:** 45 minutes

  2 tablespoons olive oil
  1 medium onion, peeled and diced
  ½ green bell pepper, seeds and ribs removed, and chopped
  2 celery ribs, rinsed, trimmed, and sliced
  2 medium redskin potatoes, scrubbed and cut into ⅓-inch dice
  1 pint fresh minced clams, drained, with juice reserved
  2 (8-ounce) bottles clam juice
  1 (14.5-ounce) can diced tomatoes, preferably petite diced, undrained
  3 tablespoons chopped fresh parsley
  1 teaspoon dried thyme
  1 bay leaf
  Salt and freshly ground black pepper to taste

1. Heat oil in a heavy 2-quart saucepan over medium-high heat. Add onion, bell pepper, and celery. Cook, stirring frequently, for 3 minutes, or until onion is translucent.
2. Add potatoes, juice from fresh clams, bottled clam juice, tomatoes, parsley, thyme, and bay leaf to the pan. Bring to a boil, reduce the heat to low, and simmer for 10 minutes, stirring occasionally, or until potatoes are tender. Add clams, bring soup back to a boil, and simmer for 5 minutes. Remove and discard bay leaf, season to taste with salt and pepper, and serve hot.

Note: The soup can be made up to 2 days in advance and refrigerated, tightly covered. Reheat over low heat, stirring occasionally, and do not allow it to boil or the clams will toughen.

Variation: While clams are traditional, here is another idea:
  • Substitute 1 pound of any firm-fleshed white fish, cut into ½-inch cubes.

Split Pea Soup with Ham

What could be better on a cold winter night? Thick, aromatic, and hearty with an undertone of smoky flavor, it's a meal in itself. If you're at the end of your ham, add the bone to the soup to achieve even more flavor.

Yield: 6–8 servings | **Active time:** 20 minutes | **Start to finish:** 1 hour

1 pound dried green split peas
2 tablespoons vegetable oil
2 medium onions, peeled and chopped
2 celery ribs, rinsed, trimmed, and chopped
1 carrot, peeled and chopped
2 garlic cloves, peeled and minced
10 cups Chicken Stock (recipe on page 33) or purchased stock
3 tablespoons chopped fresh parsley
1 teaspoon dried thyme
1 bay leaf
3/4 pound baked ham, trimmed of fat and diced
Salt and freshly ground black pepper to taste

1. Rinse peas under cold water and pick them over. Set aside.
2. Heat oil in a 3-quart saucepan over medium-high heat. Add onions, celery, carrot, and garlic, and cook, stirring frequently, for 3 minutes, or until onions are translucent. Add split peas to the pan, along with stock, parsley, thyme, and bay leaf. Bring to a boil over high heat, stirring occasionally.
3. Reduce the heat to low and simmer soup, partially covered, for 30 minutes. Add ham, and simmer for an additional 30–40 minutes, or until peas have disintegrated and soup is thick.
4. Remove and discard bay leaf, season to taste with salt and pepper, and serve.

Note: The soup can be prepared up to 3 days in advance and refrigerated, tightly covered. Reheat it, covered, over low heat, stirring frequently.

Minestrone

Every Italian soup filled with vegetables falls under the moniker of min-
estrone, and this hearty version includes some salami for flavor and
a cornucopia of healthful vegetables and beans. A tossed salad com-
pletes your meal.

Yield: 6–8 servings | **Active time:** 20 minutes | **Start to finish:** 1 hour

¼ cup olive oil
1 large onion, peeled and diced
1 large carrot, peeled and sliced
1 celery rib, rinsed, trimmed, and sliced
3 garlic cloves, peeled and minced
¼ pound Genoa salami, chopped
4 cups shredded green cabbage
5 cups Chicken Stock (recipe on page 33) or purchased stock
1 (28-ounce) can diced tomatoes, undrained
¼ cup chopped fresh parsley
1 tablespoon Italian seasoning
2 zucchini, rinsed, trimmed, and diced
1 (15-ounce) can garbanzo beans, drained and rinsed
1 (15-ounce) can red kidney beans, drained and rinsed
¼ pound small shells or other small pasta
1 (10-ounce) package frozen cut green beans, thawed
Salt and freshly ground black pepper to taste
½ cup freshly grated Parmesan cheese

1. Heat olive oil in a 3-quart saucepan over medium-high heat. Add
   onion, carrot, celery, garlic, and salami. Cook, stirring frequently, for
   3 minutes, or until onion is translucent. Add cabbage, and cook for 1
   minute.
2. Add chicken stock, tomatoes, parsley, and Italian seasoning, and
   bring to a boil over medium-high heat, stirring occasionally. Reduce
   the heat to low, and simmer soup, partially covered, for 40 minutes.
   Add zucchini, garbanzo beans, kidney beans, and simmer an additional 15 minutes.

3. While soup simmers, bring a large pot of salted water to a boil over high heat. Cook pasta according to package directions until al dente. Drain, and set aside.

4. Add pasta and green beans to soup, and season to taste with salt and pepper. Simmer for 3 minutes. Serve hot, passing Parmesan cheese separately.

Note: The soup can be prepared up to 3 days in advance and refrigerated, tightly covered. Reheat it, covered, over low heat, stirring frequently.

Variations: Like many soups, this one can have myriad ingredients added successfully:

- To make this a vegetarian soup, substitute vegetable stock for the chicken stock, and omit the salami.
- Instead of cabbage, add ½ pound chopped kale.
- Use any beans you may have in the larder as a substitution for the garbanzo and kidney beans.

Chinese Vegetable and Meatball Soup

This aromatic and delicious light soup is similar to traditional wonton soup, except it is faster to make small meatballs that cook right in the broth than it is to fill squares of pasta dough. All the vegetables you need are right here, too.

Yield: 6-8 servings | **Active time:** 20 minutes | **Start to finish:** 1 hour

MEATBALLS

- 2 tablespoons soy sauce
- 2 tablespoons cornstarch
- 3 large egg whites
- 1 tablespoon Asian sesame oil*
- 3 scallions, white parts and 3 inches of green tops, rinsed, trimmed, and chopped
- 3 tablespoons chopped fresh cilantro
- 1 tablespoon grated fresh ginger
- 2 garlic cloves, peeled and minced
- 1 pound ground pork
- ½ cup finely chopped water chestnuts
- Salt and freshly ground black pepper to taste

SOUP

- 7 cups Chicken Stock (recipe on page 33) or purchased stock
- 6 scallions, white parts and 3 inches of green tops, rinsed, trimmed, and chopped
- 2 garlic cloves, peeled and minced
- 1 tablespoon grated fresh ginger
- 2 tablespoons soy sauce
- 1 large carrot, peeled and cut into a fine julienne
- 2 cups chopped iceberg lettuce or Napa cabbage
- 1 cup thinly sliced green beans
- Salt and freshly ground black pepper to taste

1. For meatballs, mix soy sauce with cornstarch. Combine egg whites, soy sauce mixture, sesame oil, scallions, cilantro, ginger, and garlic in

* Available in the Asian aisle of most supermarkets and in specialty markets.

a mixing bowl, and whisk well. Add pork and water chestnuts, season to taste with salt and pepper, and mix well into a paste. Chill mixture for 30 minutes.

2. For soup, combine chicken stock, scallions, garlic, ginger, soy sauce, and carrot in a 3-quart saucepan, and bring to a boil over medium-high heat. Reduce the heat to low, and simmer soup, uncovered, for 10 minutes.

3. Using wet hands, form meatball mixture into 1-inch balls, and drop them into simmering soup. Cook for 7–10 minutes, or until cooked through and no longer pink. Add lettuce or cabbage and green beans, and simmer for 2 minutes. Season to taste with salt and pepper, and serve hot.

Note: The soup can be prepared up to 3 days in advance and refrigerated, tightly covered. Reheat it, covered, over low heat, stirring frequently.

Variations: To change the look and flavor of this soup, try these alterations:

- Use some rehydrated shiitake mushrooms in addition to the water chestnuts in the meatballs.
- Add some fresh spinach leaves to the broth to up the nutrient content without changing the flavor.
- Use ground turkey instead of the pork as the protein in the meatballs.

Classic French cooking is full of fancy terms used when cutting beyond the basic slice and dice. Julienne (pronounced *julie-en)* is a long, rectangular cut used for vegetables. To julienne hard vegetables like carrots or potatoes, trim them so that the sides are straight, which will make it easier to make even cuts. Slice the vegetable lengthwise, using parallel cuts of the proper thickness. Stack the slices, aligning the edges, and make parallel cuts of the same thickness through the stack.

Tex-Mex Meatball Soup

Meatball soups, called *albóndigas* in Spanish, are a popular part of Tex-Mex cooking, and this soup is a winner with the whole family. The meatballs contain some crushed tortilla chips that remain crunchy, and the flavorful broth is full of healthful vegetables.

Yield: 4–6 servings | **Active time:** 20 minutes | **Start to finish:** 45 minutes

MEATBALLS

Vegetable oil spray
1 large egg
¼ cup tomato juice
2 garlic cloves, peeled and minced
2 teaspoons ground cumin
1 teaspoon dried oregano
¾ pound ground beef chuck
½ pound ground pork
½ cup crushed tortilla chips
Salt and freshly ground black pepper to taste

SOUP

¼ cup olive oil
1 large onion, peeled and diced
2 garlic cloves, peeled and minced
2 tablespoons chili powder
6 cups Beef Stock (recipe on page 34) or purchased stock
2 (14.5-ounce) cans petite diced tomatoes, undrained
2 celery ribs, rinsed, trimmed, and sliced
2 carrots, peeled and sliced
1 (15-ounce) can kidney beans, drained and rinsed
1 cup fresh corn kernels or frozen kernels, thawed
½ cup fresh peas or frozen peas, thawed
Salt and freshly ground black pepper to taste

1. Preheat the oven to 450°F, cover a rimmed baking sheet with heavy duty aluminum foil, and spray the foil with vegetable oil spray.

2. For meatballs, combine egg, tomato juice, garlic, cumin, and oregano in medium mixing bowl, and whisk well. Add beef, pork, and tortilla chips, season to taste with salt and pepper, and mix well. Make mixture into 1-inch meatballs, and arrange meatballs on the prepared pan. Spray tops of meatballs with vegetable oil spray. Bake meatballs for 12–15 minutes.

3. For soup, while meatballs bake, heat olive oil in heavy 3-quart saucepan over medium-high heat. Add onion and garlic, and cook, stirring frequently, for 3 minutes, or until onion is translucent. Stir in chili powder, and cook for 1 minute, stirring constantly. Stir in beef stock, tomatoes, celery, and carrots.

4. Bring to a boil and simmer soup, uncovered, for 20 minutes, or until vegetables are tender. Add meatballs, kidney beans, corn, and peas to soup, and simmer for 5 minutes. Season to taste with salt and pepper, and serve immediately.

Note: The soup can be made up to 2 days in advance and refrigerated, tightly covered. Reheat it over low heat, covered.

Variations: If you like the flavors in this soup, try these additions and changes too:

- Make the meatballs from turkey, and use chicken stock instead of beef stock.
- Use any sort of canned beans in your larder; there's no reason to purchase kidney beans if you have others around.

Be careful when adding salt to dishes that contain a salted food such as tortilla chips. Chances are the meatball mixture will need very little, if any, salt because the salt from the chips is part of the mixture.

Italian Wedding Soup

Wedding soup is actually Italian-American, rather than tied to any region of Italy. It is a mistranslation of *minestra maritata* which has nothing to do with nuptials, but is a reference to the fact that green vegetables and meats go well together. Serve it with a loaf of garlic bread and your meal is complete.

Yield: 6–8 servings | **Active time:** 20 minutes | **Start to finish:** 1 hour

MEATBALLS

1 large egg
½ cup breadcrumbs
¼ cup whole milk
1 small onion, peeled and grated
2 garlic cloves, peeled and minced
½ cup freshly grated Parmesan cheese
¼ cup chopped fresh parsley
2 teaspoons Italian seasoning
1 pound ground beef
½ pound ground pork
Salt and freshly ground black pepper to taste

SOUP

8 cups Chicken Stock (recipe on page 33) or purchased stock
1 pound curly endive, rinsed, cored, and coarsely chopped
2 large eggs
½ cup freshly grated Parmesan cheese, divided
Salt and freshly ground black pepper to taste

1. For meatballs, combine egg, breadcrumbs, milk, onion, garlic, Parmesan, parsley, and Italian seasoning, and mix well. Add beef and pork, season to taste with salt and pepper, and mix well to form a paste.
2. For soup, combine chicken stock and endive in a 3-quart saucepan, and bring to a boil over medium-high heat. Reduce the heat to low, and simmer soup, uncovered, for 10 minutes.

3. Using wet hands, form meatball mixture into 1-inch balls, and drop them into simmering soup. Cook for 7–10 minutes, or until cooked through and no longer pink.
4. Whisk eggs with 2 tablespoons cheese. Stir soup and gradually add egg mixture to form thin strands. Season to taste with salt and pepper, and serve immediately, passing remaining cheese separately.

Note: The soup can be made up to 2 days in advance and refrigerated, tightly covered. Reheat it over low heat, covered.

Variations: Here are some alterations you can make to this recipe:
- If you can't find curly endive, or want a more prominent flavor, try this soup with escarole.
- Pork or turkey are equally delicious for the meatballs.

One of the purposes of browning meatballs is to get them to hold together because the exterior becomes hard. When meatballs are being poached gently in a soup such as this one without browning, you should beat the mixture well to a smooth consistency rather than handling it gently to achieve a coarser texture. The meatball mixture should be smooth before you drop the nuggets into the soup.

Tuscan White Bean Soup with Sausage

This hearty soup is relatively fast to make because I developed the recipe using canned beans. The combination of the mild beans with the hearty sausage is delicious, and a tossed salad and loaf of crusty bread are all you need for a complete meal.

Yield: 6–8 servings | **Active time:** 20 minutes | **Start to finish:** 45 minutes

1 pound bulk Italian sausage (sweet or hot)
2 large onions, peeled and diced
4 garlic cloves, peeled and minced
4 celery ribs, rinsed, trimmed, and diced
2 carrots, peeled and diced
1 (6-inch) rind from Parmesan cheese, optional
4 cups Chicken Stock (recipe on page 33) or purchased stock
3 (15-ounce) cans white beans, drained and rinsed, divided
¼ cup chopped fresh parsley
1½ teaspoons dried thyme
1 bay leaf
1 cup water
¾ pound Swiss chard, rinsed, stemmed, and thinly sliced
½ cup freshly grated Parmesan cheese
Salt and freshly ground black pepper to taste

1. Place a heavy 3-quart saucepan over medium-high heat. Add sausage, breaking up lumps with a fork. Cook, stirring frequently, for 3 minutes, or until sausage is browned and no longer pink. Remove sausage from the pan with a slotted spoon, and set aside. Discard all but 1 tablespoon sausage fat from the pan.
2. Add onions, garlic, celery, and carrots to the pan. Cook for 3 minutes, stirring frequently, or until onions are translucent. Add sausage, Parmesan rind (if using), chicken stock, ½ of beans, parsley, thyme, and bay leaf to the pan. Bring to a boil over medium heat, and simmer, partially covered, for 20 minutes, or until carrots are soft.

3. While soup simmers, combine reserved beans and water in a blender or food processor fitted with the steel blade. Puree until smooth, and stir mixture into soup.
4. Add Swiss chard to soup, and simmer for 5 minutes. Remove and discard bay leaf and Parmesan rind (if using), and stir Parmesan cheese into soup. Season to taste with salt and pepper, and serve immediately.

Note: The soup can be prepared up to 3 days in advance and refrigerated, tightly covered. Reheat it, covered, over low heat, stirring frequently.

Remember, in my kitchen nothing goes to waste! So I save the rinds from Parmesan cheese and use them for flavoring dishes such as soups and sauces. The rind will not melt into the dishes, but it will impart flavor. Remove and discard it before serving.

White Bean Soup with Ham and Spinach

I've discovered that soaking small white beans is really not a necessity as it is with other beans; they cook enough as part of the soup. Some aromatic rosemary and bright green spinach complement the ham flavoring this thick soup.

Yield: 6–8 servings | **Active time:** 15 minutes | **Start to finish:** 1¾ hours

2 tablespoons olive oil

1 medium onion, peeled and diced

1 carrot, peeled and sliced

1 celery rib, rinsed, trimmed, and sliced

3 garlic cloves, peeled and minced

1½ cups finely diced baked ham

1 pound dried small white beans, such as cannellini or navy beans

2 tablespoons fresh chopped rosemary or 1 tablespoon dried

10 cups Chicken Stock (recipe on page 33) or purchased stock

1 (10-ounce) package frozen leaf spinach, thawed and drained well

Salt and freshly ground black pepper to taste

1. Heat oil in a 3-quart saucepan over medium-high heat. Add onion, carrot, celery, garlic, and ham and cook, stirring frequently, for 5 minutes, or until vegetables begin to soften.
2. Add beans, rosemary, and chicken stock, and bring to a boil. Simmer, covered, for 1½ hours, or until beans are soft.
3. Puree soup in a food processor fitted with a steel blade or in a blender. Return soup to the saucepan, and add spinach. Simmer for 2 minutes. Season to taste with salt and pepper, and serve hot.

Note: The soup can be prepared up to 3 days in advance and refrigerated, tightly covered. Reheat it, covered, over low heat, stirring frequently.

Two Mushroom, Beef, and Barley Soup

Barley is one of the oldest grains known to man, and it's delicious in this soup. The combination of beef and woodsy mushrooms makes this soup a satisfying winter treat.

Yield: 6–8 servings | **Active time:** 20 minutes | **Start to finish:** 1½ hours

> ¼ cup dried mushrooms, such as porcini
> ½ cup boiling water
> 2 tablespoons vegetable oil
> 1 pound boneless beef chuck, rinsed and cut into ½-inch dice
> 1 large onion, peeled and diced
> 2 carrots, peeled and sliced
> 2 celery ribs, rinsed, trimmed, and sliced
> 1 pound white mushrooms, rinsed, stemmed, and sliced
> 8 cups Beef Stock (recipe on page 34) or purchased stock
> 1 cup pearled barley, rinsed well
> 3 tablespoons chopped fresh parsley
> 1 teaspoon dried thyme
> Salt and freshly ground black pepper to taste

1. Combine dried mushrooms and boiling water, pushing them down into the water. Soak for 10 minutes, then drain mushrooms, reserving soaking liquid, and chop mushrooms. Strain soaking liquid through a paper coffee filter or a paper towel. Set aside.
2. Heat oil in a 3-quart saucepan over medium-high heat. Add beef and brown well on all sides. Remove beef from the pan with a slotted spoon, and set aside. Add onion and cook, stirring frequently, for 3 minutes, or until onion is translucent.
3. Return beef to the pan, and add carrots, celery, white mushrooms, stock, barley, parsley, thyme, chopped dried mushrooms, and reserved mushroom liquid; bring to a boil over medium-high heat. Reduce heat to low, and simmer soup, covered, for 1 hour, or until beef and barley are tender. Season to taste with salt and pepper, and serve hot.

Note: The soup can be prepared up to 3 days in advance and refrigerated, tightly covered. Reheat it, covered, over low heat, stirring frequently.

Variation: Here is an idea for changing this soup:

- For the ultimate in mushroom flavor, substitute fresh portobello mushrooms for the white mushrooms if you can find them on sale.

Southwestern Chicken Vegetable Soup

This hearty chicken soup is filled with healthful vegetables and legumes. Serve it with some corn tortillas and a tossed salad.

Yield: 6–8 servings | **Active time:** 20 minutes | **Start to finish:** 20 minutes

> 2 tablespoons olive oil
> 1 large onion, peeled and diced
> 2 garlic cloves, peeled and minced
> 1 jalapeño or serrano chile, seeds and ribs removed, and finely chopped
> 1 pound boneless, skinless chicken meat, cut into ½-inch dice
> 2 carrots, peeled and diced
> 2 celery ribs, rinsed, trimmed, and sliced
> 8 cups Chicken Stock (recipe on page 33) or purchased stock
> 1 (14.5-ounce) can diced tomatoes, undrained
> 2 small zucchini, rinsed, trimmed, and diced
> 1 (15-ounce) can garbanzo beans, drained and rinsed
> ¼ cup chopped fresh cilantro
> Salt and freshly ground black pepper to taste

1. Heat oil in a 3-quart saucepan over medium-high heat. Add onion, garlic, and chile, and cook, stirring frequently, for 3 minutes, or until onion is translucent.
2. Add chicken, carrots, celery, stock, and tomatoes, and bring to a boil over medium-high heat. Reduce the heat to low, and simmer soup, covered, for 20 minutes. Add zucchini and garbanzo beans, and simmer for an additional 10 minutes, or until vegetables are tender. Stir in cilantro, season to taste with salt and pepper, and serve hot.

Note: The soup can be prepared up to 3 days in advance and refrigerated, tightly covered. Reheat it, covered, over low heat, stirring frequently.

Variations: Like all vegetable soups, this one can be personalized in many ways:

- Add some sautéed bell pepper to the mix, and substitute yellow squash for the zucchini.
- Instead of garbanzo beans, use pinto beans or kidney beans.

Chapter 4:
Fishy Business

Americans' per capita fish consumption continues to rise, and while the annual seventeen-plus pounds hardly compares with that of chicken or red meats, it's almost double what that figure was twenty years ago.

There's a good reason for this increase; fish is both versatile and healthy—and it cooks quickly. Fish is high in protein and low to moderate in fat, cholesterol, and sodium. A 3-ounce portion of fish has between 47 and 170 calories, depending on the species. Fish is an excellent source of B vitamins, iodine, phosphorus, potassium, iron, and calcium.

The most important nutrient in fish may be the omega-3 fatty acids. These are the primary polyunsaturated fatty acids found in the fat and oils of fish. They have been found to lower the levels of low-density lipoproteins (LDL, the "bad" cholesterol) and raise the levels of high-density lipoproteins (HDL, the "good" cholesterol). Fatty fish that live in cold water, such as mackerel and salmon, seem to have the most omega-3 fatty acids, although all fish have some.

SWIMMING WITH BARGAINS

You will notice that the recipes in this chapter are not written for a specific species of fish; rather, they give a description such as firm-fleshed, thick, or thin. The reason for that is that it's best to find the freshest fish at the most reasonable price rather than a specific species. The freshest fish will almost always be one that is locally caught, be it from an ocean, lake, or mountain stream.

Certain species, such as halibut, striped bass, and wild salmon, are usually much higher in price than farm-raised catfish, tilapia, cod, and flounder. But almost every fish department has a thin fillet and a thick fillet reasonably priced at all times. These recipes were developed so that a wide range of fish can be prepared.

Many fish markets also discount the "ends" of fish at an attractive price. For example, I've found small pieces of swordfish perfect for a kebab at less than half the cost of swordfish steaks. And for a treat, many markets also sell bits of smoked salmon reasonably too!

There are health concerns as well as cost reasons for specifying light tuna rather than white tuna, sometimes called albacore tuna, in these recipes. White tuna has been found to be much higher in mercury than light tuna, so light tuna is better on both scores. Feel free in any of the recipes containing canned tuna to substitute canned salmon. Almost all canned salmon is packaged complete with bones and skin, however, so some preparatory work is needed before using it in recipes.

Baked Fish with Tomatoes and Fennel

Fennel is a relatively inexpensive vegetable, and it's underutilized in cooking. It has the crunchy texture of celery, but a refreshing anise flavor. When combined with onion and tomatoes, it becomes a fast and lean sauce for fish.

Yield: 4–6 servings | **Active time:** 20 minutes | **Start to finish:** 35 minutes

- ¼ cup olive oil
- 1 large onion, peeled and thinly sliced
- 3 garlic cloves, peeled and minced
- 2 fennel bulbs, trimmed, cored, and thinly sliced
- 1 (28-ounce) can diced tomatoes, drained
- 1 cup dry white wine
- ½ cup orange juice
- 2 bay leaves
- Salt and freshly ground black pepper to taste
- 1½ pounds thick fish fillets such as cod or bass, rinsed and cut into serving-sized pieces

1. Preheat the oven to 450°F, and grease a 9x13-inch baking pan.
2. Heat olive oil in a large saucepan over medium heat. Add onion and garlic, and cook, stirring frequently, for 3 minutes, or until onion is translucent. Add fennel, and cook for 2 minutes, stirring frequently. Add tomatoes, wine, orange juice, and bay leaves to the pan. Bring to a boil, reduce the heat to low, and simmer mixture, uncovered, for 15 minutes, stirring occasionally. Season to taste with salt and pepper.
3. Transfer vegetable mixture to the prepared pan. Sprinkle fish with salt and pepper, and place fish on top of the vegetables. Bake for 10–15 minutes, or until fish is opaque. Remove and discard bay leaves, and serve immediately.

Note: The vegetable mixture can be prepared up to 2 days in advance and refrigerated, tightly covered. Reheat it over low heat to a simmer before baking the fish.

Baked Fish Provençal

Provençal is the term given to dishes that are derived from the sunny cuisine of the Provence region of southern France. Certain ingredients, such as tomatoes and olives, characterize this style of cooking, and it's extremely healthy because its base is olive oil rather than butter and cream.

Yield: 4–6 servings | **Active time:** 20 minutes | **Start to finish:** 45 minutes

> ¼ cup olive oil
> 1 large onion, peeled and thinly sliced
> 3 garlic cloves, peeled and minced
> 1 (14.5-ounce) can diced tomatoes, undrained
> 3 tablespoons chopped fresh parsley
> 1 tablespoon herbes de Provence
> 1 bay leaf
> 2 large baking potatoes, peeled and thinly sliced
> ⅓ cup chopped pitted oil-cured black olives
> Salt and freshly ground black pepper to taste
> 1½ pounds thick fish fillets, such as cod or salmon, rinsed and cut
> into serving-sized pieces

1. Preheat the oven to 350°F, and grease a 9x13-inch baking pan.
2. Heat oil in large skillet over medium-high heat. Add onion and garlic, and cook, stirring frequently, for 3 minutes, or until onion is translucent. Add tomatoes, parsley, herbes de Provence, bay leaf, potatoes, and olives to the pan. Bring to a boil, and simmer, covered, for 7–10 minutes, or until potatoes are beginning to soften. Remove and discard bay leaf, and season to taste with salt and pepper.
3. Spread ½ of mixture into the prepared pan, and top with fish. Top fish with remaining vegetable mixture. Cover the pan with aluminum foil, and bake for 25 minutes, or until potatoes are tender and fish is opaque. Serve immediately.

Note: The vegetable mixture can be prepared up to 6 hours in advance. Reheat to a simmer before adding the fish and baking the dish.

Herbed Fish and Scallion Kebabs

The combination of various citrus and herb flavors makes this a dish that appeals to many people, even some who say they do not like fish. It is also excellent at room temperature as part of a buffet dinner.

Yield: 4–6 servings | **Active time:** 15 minutes | **Start to finish:** 35 minutes

8–12 (8-inch) bamboo skewers
1½ pounds thick fish fillets, such as cod or halibut
2 tablespoons lemon juice
2 tablespoons orange juice
2 tablespoons soy sauce
3 garlic cloves, peeled and minced
3 tablespoons chopped fresh parsley
2 teaspoons herbes de Provence
Freshly ground black pepper to taste
⅓ cup olive oil
16 scallions, white parts only, rinsed and trimmed

1. Soak bamboo skewers in warm water to cover. Prepare a medium-hot gas or charcoal grill, or preheat the oven broiler.
2. Rinse fish, and cut into 1-inch cubes. Combine lemon juice, orange juice, soy sauce, garlic, parsley, herbes de Provence, and pepper in a heavy resealable plastic bag, and mix well. Add oil, and mix well again. Add fish and scallions, and stir to coat evenly. Allow to marinate for 15 minutes at room temperature, turning the bag occasionally.
3. Thread fish and scallions onto 2 parallel skewers. Grill kebabs, uncovered if using a charcoal grill, for 1½ minutes per side for a total of 10 minutes, or until fish is no longer translucent. Serve immediately.

Note: The marinade can be made up to 1 day in advance and refrigerated, tightly covered.

Fish Fillets Almandine

This is an easy version of the classic French dish; the fillets are layered with rice and a mushroom cream sauce in the center rather than laboriously rolling each one. The few almonds give the buttery fish and filling some textural interest.

Yield: 4-6 servings | **Active time:** 20 minutes | **Start to finish:** 40 minutes

$^3/_4$ cup long grain white rice

$^1/_2$ cup sliced almonds

4 tablespoons ($^1/_2$ stick) unsalted butter, divided

1 small onion, peeled and diced

2 garlic cloves, peeled and minced

$^1/_4$ pound mushrooms, stemmed and thinly sliced

$^1/_4$ cup all-purpose flour

2 cups whole milk

3 tablespoons chopped fresh parsley

$^1/_2$ teaspoon dried thyme

Salt and freshly ground black pepper to taste

$1^1/_2$ pounds thin fish fillets, such as tilapia or flounder

$^1/_4$ cup dry sherry

$^1/_2$ cup grated Swiss cheese

1. Preheat the oven to 350°F, and grease a 9x13-inch baking pan.
2. Bring a large pot of salted water to a boil. Add rice and boil over medium heat, uncovered, for 15-18 minutes, or until rice is almost cooked through. Drain, and place rice in a mixing bowl. Place almonds on ungreased baking sheet, and toast in the oven for 4-6 minutes, or until lightly brown. Remove almonds from the oven, and add them to the mixing bowl.
3. Heat 2 tablespoons butter in skillet over medium-high heat. Add onion and garlic, and cook, stirring frequently, for 2 minutes. Add mushrooms, and cook, stirring frequently, for 3-5 minutes, or until mushrooms are soft. Scrape mixture into mixing bowl with rice.
4. Heat remaining 2 tablespoons butter in saucepan over low heat. Add flour, and cook, stirring constantly, for 2 minutes. Whisk in milk, and bring to a boil over medium heat, whisking constantly. Reduce the heat to low, and simmer sauce for 2 minutes. Stir in parsley and thyme, and season to taste with salt and pepper. Stir $^2/_3$ cup sauce into rice mixture.

5. Increase the oven temperature to 400°F. Lay ½ of fish in the prepared pan, and top with rice mixture. Top rice with remaining fish. Cover the pan with aluminum foil, and bake for 10 minutes. While fish bakes, combine remaining sauce and sherry, and simmer for 3 minutes.

6. Remove fish from the oven, spoon ½ cup sauce over fish, and sprinkle with cheese. Bake fish, uncovered, for an additional 10 minutes, or until fish is opaque. Serve immediately, passing remaining sauce separately.

Note: The rice mixture and sauce can be made up to 2 days in advance and refrigerated, tightly covered. Reheat both in a microwave oven or in a saucepan over low heat before layering with the fish and baking the dish.

Variations: Here are some other ways to enjoy this dish:
- Substitute 1 (10-ounce) package frozen mixed vegetables, thawed, for the mushrooms.
- Substitute 1½ cups bread stuffing cubes, sprinkled with ½ cup milk, for the cooked rice.

Fish Pot Pie

Pot pies are the quintessentially American way to enjoy food; the protein is cooked with assorted vegetables in an herbed cream sauce and then nestled beneath a crispy crust. This one made with fish is just delicious, and very easy to make.

Yield: 4–6 servings | **Active time:** 20 minutes | **Start to finish:** 1 hour

    4 tablespoons (½ stick) unsalted butter, divided
    1 medium onion, peeled and diced
    2 carrots, peeled, and thinly sliced
    2 redskin potatoes, scrubbed and cut into ½-inch dice
    1 cup dry white wine
    1 cup Seafood Stock (recipe on page 36) or bottled clam juice
    1 bay leaf
    3 tablespoons all-purpose flour
    1 cup half-and-half
    2 tablespoons chopped fresh parsley
    1 teaspoon dried thyme
    Salt and freshly ground black pepper to taste
    1 pound firm fleshed fish, cut into 1-inch cubes
    1 cup frozen peas, thawed
    1 Basic Pie Crust (recipe on page 227) or purchased pie crust sheet
    1 large egg, lightly beaten

1. Preheat the oven to 400°F.
2. Melt 2 tablespoons butter in a large skillet over medium-high heat. Add onion and cook, stirring frequently, for 3 minutes, or until onion is translucent. Add carrots, potatoes, wine, stock or clam juice, and bay leaf to pan. Bring to a boil, then reduce the heat to low and cook vegetables, uncovered, for 10 minutes, or until potatoes are almost tender. Remove and discard bay leaf. Strain and reserve cooking liquid.
3. Melt remaining 2 tablespoons butter in a small saucepan, and stir in flour. Cook over low heat, stirring constantly, for 2 minutes. Whisk in reserved cooking liquid, half-and-half, parsley, and thyme. Bring to a boil, whisking constantly, and simmer sauce for 2 minutes. Season to taste with salt and pepper.

4. Combine sauce, vegetable mixture, fish, and peas in round 2-quart casserole. Cover the pan with aluminum foil, and bake for 20 minutes. Remove casserole from the oven, and fit sheet of piecrust over the top, crimping the edges, and trimming off any excess dough. Brush crust with beaten egg, and cut 6 (1-inch) slits to allow steam to escape. Bake pie, uncovered, for 30 minutes, or until crust is brown. Serve immediately.

Note: The vegetable mixture and sauce can be prepared up to 1 day in advance and refrigerated, tightly covered. Do not add seafood to the vegetables and sauce mixture until just before baking, and add 15 minutes to initial baking time if chilled.

Variations: Here are some other ideas for pot pies:
- Substitute 1 pound cooked chicken or turkey for the fish.
- Substitute 3 (6-ounce) cans tuna, drained and broken into chunks, for the fish.

Crimping, sometimes referred to as fluting, means pinching or pressing two pastry edges together, thereby sealing the dough while forming a decorative edge with fingers, fork or some other utensil. The pastry for a single-crust pie is crimped by turning it under to form a ridge, then shaping the raised edge into a fancy pattern.

Creole Fish

This is a dish I serve a lot in the summer because it's as good at room temperature as it is hot. It has all the flavors of Louisiana, and is very easy to make.

Yield: 4–6 servings | **Active time:** 15 minutes | **Start to finish:** 30 minutes

1½ pounds thin fish fillets, such as flounder or tilapia
3 tablespoons olive oil
1 large onion, peeled and finely chopped
2 celery ribs, rinsed, trimmed, and finely chopped
3 garlic cloves, peeled and minced
1 green bell pepper, seeds and ribs removed, and finely chopped
½ cup Seafood Stock (recipe on page 36) or bottled clam juice
½ cup dry white wine
1 (14.5-ounce) can diced tomatoes, undrained
1 (15-ounce) can tomato sauce
¼ cup chopped fresh parsley
½ teaspoon dried thyme
1 bay leaf
Salt and hot red pepper sauce to taste

1. Rinse fish, cut into serving-size pieces, if necessary, and set aside.
2. Heat oil in a large skillet over medium-high heat. Add onion, celery, garlic, and green pepper. Cook, stirring frequently, for 3 minutes, or until onion is translucent. Add stock or clam juice, wine, tomatoes, tomato sauce, parsley, thyme, and bay leaf. Bring to a boil, reduce the heat to low, and simmer sauce, uncovered, for 10 minutes.
3. Add fish to the skillet, and poach fish, partially covered, for 5–6 minutes, depending on thickness, or until cooked through.
4. Remove fish from the pan with a slotted spatula, and keep warm. Raise the heat to high and reduce sauce by ⅓, stirring frequently. Season to taste with salt and red pepper sauce, and serve immediately or at room temperature.

Note: The sauce can be prepared up to 2 days in advance and refrigerated, tightly covered. Reheat it to a simmer before cooking the fish.

Variations: Here are some other ways to enjoy this sauce:
- Brown chicken pieces in the oil before cooking the vegetables, and cook chicken, covered, for 20-25 minutes, or until cooked through and no longer pink.
- Brown boneless pork chops in the oil before cooking the vegetables, and cook pork chops for 15-20 minutes, or until cooked through and tender.

To poach is to cook food gently in liquid that is just at the boiling point and the liquid is barely simmering. This way of cooking preserves tenderness in what's being cooked, be it an egg or a fish steak.

Linguine with White Clam Sauce

Pre-minced fresh clams are one of the great convenience foods on the market because they are so easy to use and so economical. One pint can serve a number of people when turned into this robust sauce, which is a classic of northern Italian cooking.

Yield: 4–6 servings | **Active time:** 15 minutes | **Start to finish:** 35 minutes

1 pound linguine
1 pint fresh minced clams
¼ cup olive oil
1 small onion, peeled and chopped
6 garlic cloves, peeled and minced
1 (8-ounce) bottle clam juice
¾ cup dry white wine
¼ cup chopped fresh parsley
2 teaspoons Italian seasoning
¼ teaspoon red pepper flakes or to taste
2 ripe plum tomatoes, rinsed, cored, seeded, and diced
Salt and freshly ground black pepper to taste
½ cup freshly grated Parmesan cheese

1. Bring a large pot of salted water to a boil. Add pasta, and cook according to package directions until al dente. Drain, and set aside. Place clams in a colander over a mixing bowl. Press with the back of a spoon to extract as much liquid as possible. Refrigerate clams if not proceeding immediately.

2. Heat olive oil in a heavy saucepan over medium-high heat. Add onion and garlic and cook, stirring frequently, for 3 minutes, or until onion is translucent. Add reserved clam juice, bottled clam juice, wine, parsley, Italian seasoning, and red pepper flakes. Bring to a boil, stirring occasionally. Simmer sauce, uncovered, for 20 minutes, or until reduced by ½.

3. Add tomatoes and clams to sauce. Bring to a boil, and simmer for 5 minutes, stirring occasionally. Season to taste with salt and pepper. Add pasta to sauce, and serve immediately, passing Parmesan cheese separately.

Note: The sauce can be prepared up to 2 days in advance and refrigerated, tightly covered. Reheat it over low heat, and cook the pasta just prior to serving.

Variations: This easy sauce is open to many interpretations:
- While white wine is the usual choice for cooking with fish, you can also use red wine if you have it around.
- Substitute $3/4$ pound firm-fleshed white fish, such as tilapia or cod, finely chopped , for the clams.

Foods like clams cook so quickly that they should always be added to dishes at the end of cooking time; however, a sauce should not be seasoned until after they're cooked because they will give off liquid into the food.

Spanish Fish

It doesn't get much easier than this recipe; there are just a few ingredients and it's on the table in a matter of minutes. I usually serve it over rice or with a loaf of crusty bread to enjoy every drop of the garlicky sauce.

Yield: 4–6 servings | **Active time:** 15 minutes | **Start to finish:** 15 minutes

1½ pounds firm-fleshed white fish fillets
½ cup olive oil
6 garlic cloves, peeled and minced
2 tablespoons smoked Spanish paprika
3 tablespoons chopped fresh parsley
Salt and red pepper flakes to taste

1. Rinse fish, pat dry with paper towels, and cut fish into ¾-inch cubes.
2. Heat oil in a large skillet over medium-high heat. Add garlic and paprika, and cook for 1 minute, stirring constantly. Add fish and parsley, and cook for 2 minutes, uncovered, or until fish is opaque. Season to taste with salt and red pepper flakes, and serve immediately.

Note: The fish can be prepared up to 3 hours in advance, and served at room temperature.

Lowcountry Fish and Rice

Lowcountry refers to the area between Charleston, South Carolina, and Savannah, Georgia, which was the first great rice-producing area. This flavorful combination of rice, vegetables, and lean fish is quick to make, too.

Yield: 4–6 servings | **Active time:** 15 minutes | **Start to finish:** 30 minutes

  3 tablespoons olive oil
  1 medium onion, peeled and diced
  3 garlic cloves, peeled and minced
  ½ green bell pepper, seeds and ribs removed, and diced
  1½ cups long-grain white rice
  3 cups Seafood Stock (recipe on page 36) or bottled clam juice
  1 teaspoon dried oregano
  1 teaspoon dried thyme
  1 bay leaf
  1 cup frozen peas, thawed
  1 pound white firm-fleshed fish fillets, cut into 1-inch cubes
  Salt and freshly ground black pepper to taste

1. Heat oil in a large saucepan over medium-high heat. Add onion, garlic, and bell pepper, and cook, stirring frequently, for 3 minutes, or until onion is translucent. Add rice, and cook for 2 minutes, stirring frequently.

2. Add stock, oregano, thyme, and bay leaf to the pan, and bring to a boil. Cover the pan, reduce the heat to low, and cook rice for 12–15 minutes, or until liquid is almost absorbed. Remove and discard bay leaf, add peas and fish to the pan, and cook for 5–7 minutes, or until fish is cooked through and rice is soft. Season to taste with salt and pepper, and serve immediately.

Note: The dish can be prepared up to 1 day in advance and refrigerated, tightly covered. Reheat, covered, in a 350°F oven for 15–20 minutes, or until hot.

Spicy Southwest Fish with Pinto Beans

Mexico has a long coastline on both shores, and this dish is inspired by some authentic preparations from Veracruz. It's made with canned beans, so it's on the table in minutes, and is perfect served with white rice and a tossed salad.

Yield: 4–6 servings | **Active time:** 15 minutes | **Start to finish:** 30 minutes

2 tablespoons olive oil
2 medium onions, peeled and diced
5 garlic cloves, peeled and minced
2 jalapeño or serrano chiles, seeds and ribs removed, and finely chopped
1 tablespoon ground cumin
1 (14.5-ounce) can diced tomatoes, drained
2 (15-ounce) cans pinto beans, drained and rinsed
1 ½ cups Seafood Stock (recipe on page 36) or bottled clam juice
3 tablespoons chopped fresh cilantro
½ teaspoon dried thyme
1 pound white firm-fleshed fish fillets, cut into 1-inch cubes
Salt and freshly ground black pepper to taste

1. Heat oil in a large saucepan over medium-high heat. Add onion, garlic, and chiles, and cook, stirring frequently, for 3 minutes, or until onions are translucent. Add cumin, and cook for 1 minute, stirring constantly.

2. Add tomatoes, beans, stock or clam juice, cilantro, and thyme to the pan. Bring to a boil, reduce the heat to low, and simmer for 10 minutes. Add fish to the pan, and cook for 5–7 minutes, or until fish is cooked through. Season to taste with salt and pepper, and serve immediately.

Note: The bean mixture can be prepared 1 day in advance and refrigerated, tightly covered. Reheat it over low heat in a saucepan. Cook the fish just prior to serving.

Variations: Here are some other ways to enjoy these spicy beans:
- To make it a vegetarian dish, substitute 1-inch cubes of firm tofu for the fish, and use vegetable stock in the bean mixture.
- Use 1-inch cubes of boneless poultry instead of fish, along with chicken stock, and cook chicken for 12–15 minutes, or until cooked through and no longer pink.

Be careful when cooking hot chiles that the steam from the pan doesn't get in your eyes. The potent oils in the peppers can be transmitted in the vapor.

Fish, Corn, and Pea Risotto

The delicate flavors of bright green peas and sweet yellow corn are wonderful foils to the tender fish cubes in this creamy rice dish. Serve it with a tossed salad.

Yield: 4–6 servings | **Active time:** 15 minutes | **Start to finish:** 35 minutes

1 (1-pound) package frozen peas, thawed
2½ cups Vegetable Stock (recipe on page 35) or purchased stock, divided
3 tablespoons unsalted butter
3 tablespoons olive oil
1 medium onion, peeled and chopped
1 garlic clove, peeled and minced
1⅓ cups Arborio rice
⅔ cup dry white wine
3 tablespoons chopped fresh parsley
1 teaspoon dried thyme
1 pound white firm-fleshed fish fillet, rinsed and cut into ½-inch cubes
1 cup fresh corn kernels or frozen corn kernels, thawed
½ cup freshly grated Parmesan cheese
Salt and freshly ground black pepper to taste

1. Combine 1 cup peas with ½ cup stock in a food processor fitted with a steel blade or in a blender. Puree until smooth, and set aside.
2. Heat butter and olive oil in a heavy 2-quart saucepan over medium-high heat. Add onion and garlic. Cook, stirring frequently, for 3 minutes, or until onion is translucent. Stir in rice, making sure grains are all coated with fat.
3. Raise the heat to high and add wine, parsley, and thyme. Cook, stirring constantly, until wine has almost evaporated. Add remaining stock and bring to a boil. Cover the pan, reduce the heat to a simmer, and cook rice for 15 minutes, or until liquid is almost absorbed, stirring occasionally.

4. Stir in pea puree, remaining peas, fish, and corn. Cook for an additional 5–7 minutes, or until fish is cooked through, stirring gently. Remove the pan from the heat, and stir in Parmesan cheese. Season to taste with salt and pepper, and serve immediately.

Note: You can go as far as step 3 up to 4 hours in advance. Bring the mixture back to a simmer before continuing.

Arborio, pronounced *ar-BORE-e-oh*, is a species of rice with short kernels and a very high starch content. It's used for risotto because the starch gives the finished dish its creamy appearance.

Salade Niçoise

Here is a light salad from the sunny coast of the Mediterranean that you could actually gather from the supermarket salad bar! The only "cooking" involved is a few vegetables, and it's ready to eat in minutes.

Yield: 4–6 servings | **Active time:** 10 minutes | **Start to finish:** 25 minutes

¾ pound small new potatoes, scrubbed and quartered
½ pound green beans
4–6 cups chopped iceberg or romaine lettuce
2 (6-ounce) cans light tuna, drained
3 hard boiled eggs, peeled and sliced
½ cup pitted oil-cured black olives, halved
3 ripe plum tomatoes, rinsed, cored, and sliced
½ cup Mustard Herb Vinaigrette (recipe on page 13) or purchased vinaigrette dressing

1. Bring a large pot of salted water to a boil over high heat. Add potatoes and cook for 10–12 minutes, or until tender. Add green beans to the pan and cook for 2 minutes. Drain vegetables, and plunge into ice water to stop the cooking action. Drain vegetables, and set aside.

2. Arrange lettuce on a serving platter or individual plates, and arrange potatoes, beans, tuna, eggs, olives, and tomatoes on top. Drizzle with dressing, and serve immediately.

Note: The vegetables can be cooked up to 2 days in advance and refrigerated, tightly covered. Arrange and dress the salad just prior to serving.

Italian White Bean and Tuna Salad

This hearty salad is delicious for a summer supper, and can also be used as part of an Italian antipasto table. The dressing is merely the oil from the tuna with some lemon juice, and if you substitute canned beans it's ever so speedy.

Yield: 4–6 servings | **Active time:** 10 minutes | **Start to finish:** 1½ hours

2 cups dried white navy beans
2 quarts water
1 teaspoon salt
½ teaspoon freshly ground black pepper
2 garlic cloves, peeled and smashed
2 (6-ounce) cans light tuna packed in oil
⅓ cup chopped fresh parsley
4 scallions, white parts and 3 inches of green tops, rinsed, trimmed, and chopped
3 tablespoons lemon juice
Salt and freshly ground black pepper to taste

1. Rinse beans under cold water. Combine beans, water, salt, pepper, and garlic in large saucepan, and bring to a boil over high heat. Reduce the heat to low, and simmer beans, covered, for 45 minutes to 1 hour, or until cooked through but not mushy. Remove and discard garlic cloves, drain beans, and chill for 45 minutes.
2. Add tuna to beans with oil from the cans, breaking tuna up into chunks with a fork. Add parsley, scallions, and lemon juice to the salad, and mix gently. Season to taste with salt and pepper, and serve.

Note: The salad can be prepared up to 3 days in advance and refrigerated, tightly covered with plastic wrap. Allow it to reach room temperature before serving.

Updated Tuna Noodle Casserole

The basic concept of this homey classic is great; what had marred it was the execution with chemical-laden canned soup! But it's fast and easy to make your own cream sauce, and the fresh mushrooms are a great addition.

Yield: 4–6 servings | **Active time:** 15 minutes | **Start to finish:** 45 minutes

6 ounces medium egg noodles

5 tablespoons unsalted butter, divided

1 medium onion, peeled and diced

2 celery ribs, rinsed, trimmed, and diced

½ pound mushrooms, wiped with a damp paper towel, stemmed, and diced

¼ cup all-purpose flour

2 cups whole milk

Salt and freshly ground black pepper to taste

2 (6-ounce) cans light tuna, drained and broken into chunks

1 (5-ounce) bag potato chips, crushed

1. Preheat the oven to 375°F, and grease a 9x13-inch baking pan. Bring a large pot of salted water to a boil, and cook noodles according to package directions. Drain, and return noodles to the pot.

2. Melt 2 tablespoons butter in a large skillet over medium-high heat. Add onion, celery, and mushrooms. Cook, stirring frequently, for 5–7 minutes, or until celery softens. Remove the skillet from the heat and set aside. Add vegetables to the pot with noodles.

3. Melt remaining butter in saucepan over low heat. Stir in flour and cook, stirring constantly, for 2 minutes. Slowly whisk in milk, and bring to a boil over medium heat, whisking constantly. Simmer 1 minute, and season to taste with salt and pepper. Pour sauce into the pot with noodles, and gently fold in tuna.

4. Scrape mixture into the prepared pan, level top with rubber spatula, and sprinkle with potato chips. Cover pan with aluminum foil, and bake for 10 minutes. Remove foil, and bake an additional 20 minutes, or until hot and bubbly. Serve immediately.

Note: The dish can be prepared for baking up to 2 days in advance and refrigerated, tightly covered. Add 10 minutes to covered baking time if the dish is chilled, and do not sprinkle with potato chip crumbs until just before baking.

Variations: Here are some other ways to enjoy this dish:

- Add ½ green or red bell pepper, chopped, to the skillet with the other vegetables.
- Substitute canned salmon, bones and skin discarded, for the tuna.
- Substitute ¾ pound cooked chicken or turkey for the tuna.

Pasta with Tuna and Olive Sauce

Canned tuna makes a wonderful addition to a zesty tomato sauce to serve over pasta. A green salad is all you need to complete the meal.

Yield: 4–6 servings | **Active time:** 15 minutes | **Start to finish:** 30 minutes

  ¾ pound linguine or other thin pasta
  2 tablespoons olive oil
  1 small onion, peeled and diced
  3 garlic cloves, peeled and minced
  1 celery rib, rinsed, trimmed, and thinly sliced
  1 (28-ounce) can crushed tomatoes in tomato puree
  ½ cup dry white wine
  ¾ cup pimiento-stuffed green olives, chopped
  ¼ cup chopped fresh parsley
  1 tablespoon Italian seasoning
  1 bay leaf
  2 (6-ounce) cans light tuna, drained and broken into chunks
  Salt and freshly ground black pepper to taste
  ½ cup freshly grated Parmesan cheese

1. Bring a large pot of salted water to a boil. Add pasta and cook according to package directions until al dente. Drain, and set aside.
2. While water heats, heat oil in skillet over medium-high heat. Add onion, garlic, and celery. Cook, stirring frequently, for 3 minutes, or until onion is translucent. Add tomatoes, wine, olives, parsley, Italian seasoning, and bay leaf. Bring to a boil, reduce the heat to medium, and simmer sauce, uncovered, for 15 minutes. Season to taste with salt and pepper, and stir in cooked pasta and tuna. Cover pan, and cook for 2 minutes.
3. Remove and discard bay leaf. Serve immediately, sprinkling individual servings with Parmesan cheese.

Note: The sauce can be made up to 2 days in advance and refrigerated, tightly covered. Reheat it over low heat, covered.

Tuna Melt Niçoise

A tuna melt is basically a combination of a tuna salad sandwich and a grilled cheese sandwich; the tuna is covered with cheese and popped under the broiler to melt the cheese. In this recipe, olives give the tuna salad more flavor and texture.

Yield: 4–6 servings | **Active time:** 10 minutes | **Start to finish:** 12 minutes

  2 (6-ounce) cans light tuna, drained and flaked
  $\frac{1}{2}$ cup mayonnaise
  2 celery ribs, rinsed, trimmed, and chopped
  $\frac{1}{3}$ cup pitted Kalamata, or other pitted brine-cured black olives, chopped
  2 tablespoons chopped fresh parsley
  2 tablespoons lemon juice
  Freshly ground black pepper to taste
  4–6 slices rye bread, lightly toasted
  1 cup grated sharp cheddar cheese

1. Preheat an oven broiler, and cover a baking sheet with heavy duty foil.
2. Combine tuna, mayonnaise, celery, olives, parsley, lemon juice, and pepper in medium mixing bowl. Stir well.
3. Place toast slices on baking sheet and divide tuna mixture between them. Spread tuna evenly, and top with grated cheese. Broil sandwiches 6 inches from broiling element for 2 minutes, or until cheese is melted and bubbly. Serve immediately.

Note: The tuna salad can be prepared up to 2 days in advance and refrigerated, tightly covered.

Peppers Stuffed with Tuna and Rice

This is a very pretty dish to serve; the rice, vegetables, and tuna are contained in cooked bell peppers, which adds to the dish's healthful nutrient content. The filling is creamy from the addition of Swiss cheese, yet it remains light.

Yield: 4–6 servings | **Active time:** 15 minutes | **Start to finish:** 50 minutes

4–6 green bell peppers
2 cups water
3 tablespoons tomato paste
¼ cup chopped fresh parsley
1 teaspoon dried thyme
1 cup long-grain white rice
½ cup grated Swiss cheese
2 tablespoons unsalted butter
1 small onion, peeled and diced
2 garlic cloves, peeled and minced
1 (10-ounce) package frozen mixed vegetables, thawed
2 (6-ounce) cans light tuna, drained and broken into chunks
Salt and freshly ground black pepper to taste

1. Preheat the oven to 350°F, and grease a 9x13-inch baking pan.
2. Bring a large pot of salted water to a boil. Cut off top ½ inch of peppers, and reserve. Scoop out seeds and ribs with your hands. Discard stems, and chop flesh from pepper tops. Blanch peppers for 5 minutes, then remove them from the pan with tongs, and place them in a bowl of ice water to stop the cooking action. Invert peppers onto paper towels, and set aside.
3. Combine water, tomato paste, parsley, and thyme in a saucepan, and stir well to dissolve tomato paste. Bring to a boil over high heat, and add rice. Reduce the heat to low, and simmer rice, covered, for 15–20 minutes, or until tender and liquid is evaporated. Stir in cheese, and set aside.

4. While rice cooks, heat butter in small skillet over medium-high heat. Add onion and garlic, and cook, stirring frequently, for 3 minutes, or until onion is translucent. Stir vegetable mixture, frozen mixed vegetables, tuna, salt, and pepper into rice.
5. Cut small slice off bottoms of peppers so they sit securely. Spoon tuna mixture into peppers, and place them in the prepared pan. Cover the pan with aluminum foil, and bake peppers for 20–25 minutes, or until peppers are soft. Serve immediately.

Note: The peppers can be prepared for baking up to 2 days in advance and refrigerated, tightly covered. Add 10 minutes to the baking time if chilled.

Blanching is a preliminary cooking of green vegetables and some fruits. The food is plunged into rapidly boiling water for a predetermined amount of time, and then removed and plunged into ice water for another minute to stop the cooking process. For vegetables, it sets the color and makes a nice tender-crisp texture; for fruits such as peaches and tomatoes, it facilitates peeling them because the skins then slide off.

Pasta with Tuna and Dill

Dill is an herb used with many fish dishes; it has a refreshing aroma and light flavor that does not overwhelm delicate fish. Mushrooms and peas add their own mild flavor and pleasing color to this sauce, too.

Yield: 4–6 servings | **Active time:** 15 minutes | **Start to finish:** 25 minutes

> ³/₄ pound small shells or gemelli pasta
> 4 tablespoons (½ stick) unsalted butter, divided
> 1 tablespoon olive oil
> 1 small onion, peeled and chopped
> ½ pound mushrooms, wiped with a damp paper towel, stemmed, and sliced
> 3 tablespoons all-purpose flour
> 2 cups Seafood Stock (recipe on page 36) or bottled clam juice
> ⅓ cup half-and-half
> 3 tablespoons chopped fresh dill
> 1 (10-ounce) package frozen peas, thawed
> 2 (6-ounce) cans light tuna, drained and broken into chunks
> Salt and freshly ground black pepper to taste

1. Bring a large pot of salted water to a boil. Cook pasta according to package directions until al dente, drain, and return pasta to the pot.
2. Heat 1 tablespoon butter and oil in a medium skillet over medium-high heat. Add onion and mushrooms, and cook, stirring frequently, for 3–5 minutes, or until mushrooms are soft. Scrape mixture into the pot with pasta.
3. Reduce the heat to low, and add remaining 3 tablespoons butter to the skillet. Stir in flour, and cook, stirring constantly, for 2 minutes. Whisk in stock or clam juice and half-and-half, and bring to a boil over medium heat, stirring occasionally. Add dill, and simmer 2 minutes. Stir sauce into pasta, and add in peas and tuna. Season to taste with salt and pepper, reheat if necessary over low heat, and serve immediately.

Note: The sauce can be prepared up to 2 days in advance and refrigerated, tightly covered. Reheat over low heat, and cook the pasta just prior to serving.

Variation: Dill and peas are what enliven this cream sauce, so try this, too:
- Substitute 2 cups diced cooked chicken or turkey for the tuna, and use chicken stock.

Chapter 5:
Poultry with Panache

Americans' consumption of chicken more than doubled during the past 30 years, and continues to rise. And it's relatively inexpensive, which is why this is such a long chapter.

What have risen the most rapidly, however, are sales of boneless, skinless chicken breasts, which are *not* inexpensive, unless you find them on sale. And chances are you already have dozens of recipes on how to prepare them. So in this chapter you'll find ways to prepare a whole, cut-up chicken and a few for less expensive chicken thighs.

One of the most economical ways to enjoy chicken is by roasting a whole 5–7-pound bird; the percentage of edible meat to bones is the best, and unless you have a large family, a single large roasting chicken will serve as the basis for two meals. The first is the chicken itself, and the second is one of the many recipes in this chapter made with already cooked chicken or turkey; in those recipes the two birds are interchangeable.

COOK IT CORRECTLY

While rules have been changing for pork in the past few years, chicken must still be cooked to an internal temperature of 180°F to ensure that there's no chance for microorganisms to survive. The best way to test the temperature is to use an instant-read meat thermometer.

When the thickest part of the chicken is probed, the reading should be 180°F. But if you don't want to take the temperature of every piece of chicken, here are the visual signals: The chicken is tender when poked with the tip of a paring knife, there is not a hint of pink even near the bones, and the juices run clear. Always test the dark meat before the white meat. Dark meat takes slightly longer to cook, so if the thighs are the proper temperature, you know the breasts will be fine.

CUTTING WITH CUNNING

Just look at the range of prices for chicken in the supermarket. Those pieces least processed—the whole chickens—are always the lowest in cost per pound. Then there are the legs and thighs or leg quarters, which can sometimes be even less expensive than a whole bird.

It is far more economical to purchase a whole chicken and cut it up yourself, rather than buying one already cut. There are also times that your choice of chicken pieces, such as thighs, isn't available, and you can always cut up a few chickens to glean the parts for that meal and freeze what's left; another benefit is that you can save the scraps and freeze them to keep you "stocked up" for soups and sauces. Here are some methods of chicken cutting you should know:

- **Cutting up a whole raw chicken.** Start by breaking back the wings until the joints snap, then use the boning knife to cut through the ball joints and detach the wings. When holding the chicken on its side, you will see a natural curve outlining the boundary between the breast and the leg/thigh quarters. Use sharp kitchen shears and cut along this line. Cut the breast in half by scraping away the meat from the breast bone, and using a small paring knife to remove the wish bone. Cut away the breast bone using the shears, and save it for stock. Divide the thigh/leg quarters by turning the pieces over and finding the joint joining them. Cut through the joint and sever the leg from the thigh.

- **Boning raw chicken breasts.** If possible, buy the chicken breasts whole rather than split. Pull the skin off with your fingers, and then make an incision on either side of the breast bone, cutting down until you feel the bone resisting the knife. Treating one side at a time, place the blade of your boning knife against the carcass, and scrape away the meat. You will then have two pieces—the large fillet, and the small tenderloin. To trim the fillet, cut away any fat. Some recipes will tell you to pound the breast to an even thickness, so it will cook evenly and quickly. Place the breast between two sheets of plastic wrap, and pound with the smooth side of a meat mallet or the bottom of a small, heavy skillet or saucepan.

  If you have a favorite veal scallop recipe, and want to substitute chicken or turkey, pound it very thin—to a thickness of $1/4$ inch. Otherwise, your goal is to pound the thicker portion so that it lies and cooks evenly. To trim the tenderloin, secure the tip of the tendon that will be visible with your free hand. Using a paring knife, scrape down the tendon, and the meat will push away.

Basic Oven-Fried Chicken

Using this easy method, chicken emerges from the oven with skin as crisp as if it was deep-fried on top of the stove, but there's no mess! And you can read a book while it bakes, or prepare the rest of dinner.

Yield: 4–6 servings | **Active time:** 10 minutes | **Start to finish:** 35 minutes

> 1 (3½–4-pound) frying chicken, cut into serving pieces
> 1 cup buttermilk
> 2 large eggs, lightly beaten
> 1½ cups finely crushed corn flakes
> ½ cup plain breadcrumbs
> 1 cup vegetable oil, divided
> 3 tablespoons Cajun seasoning
> Salt and freshly ground black pepper to taste

1. Preheat the oven to 400°F, and place a 10x14-inch baking pan in the oven as it heats. Rinse chicken and pat dry with paper towels.
2. Combine buttermilk and eggs in a shallow bowl, and whisk well. Combine crushed corn flakes, breadcrumbs, 2 tablespoons oil, Cajun seasoning, salt, and pepper in a second large bowl, and mix well.
3. Dip chicken pieces into buttermilk mixture, shake off excess, and dip pieces into breadcrumb mixture, coating all sides. Set aside.
4. Add remaining oil to hot baking dish, and heat for 3 minutes. Add chicken pieces and turn gently with tongs to coat all sides with oil. Bake for a total of 25 minutes, turning pieces gently with tongs after 15 minutes, or until chicken is cooked through and no longer pink, and the white meat registers 160°F and dark meat registers 165°F on an instant read thermometer. Remove chicken from the pan, and pat with paper towels. Serve immediately.

Note: The chicken can be prepared for baking up to 6 hours in advance and refrigerated, tightly covered.

Variations: Here are some other coatings:
- Use seasoned Italian breadcrumbs, and add ¼ cup freshly grated Parmesan cheese to the mixture.
- Use rice cereal in place of the corn flakes.
- Use fluffy panko breadcrumbs, and season them with herbes de Provence.
- Substitute smoked Spanish paprika for the Cajun seasoning, and season egg mixture to taste with salt and pepper.

Chicken and Sausage Jambalaya

Jambalaya is a staple of Louisiana cooking, where culinary traditions of France, Spain, Italy, and the New World, among others, blended. Jambalaya was the local adaptation of the Spanish rice dish, paella, and became a favorite among the Cajuns, French transplants who settled in the Louisiana bayous.

Yield: 4–6 servings | **Active time:** 20 minutes | **Start to finish:** 55 minutes

1 (3½–4-pound) frying chicken, cut into serving pieces, with each breast half cut in half

Salt and freshly ground black pepper to taste

3 tablespoons olive oil

½ pound kielbasa or other smoked sausage, cut into ½-inch-thick slices

2 celery ribs, rinsed, trimmed, and chopped

1 large onion, peeled and diced

½ green bell pepper, seeds and ribs removed, and diced

4 garlic cloves, peeled and minced

2 (5-ounce) packages yellow rice

1½ cups Chicken Stock (recipe on page 33) or purchased stock

2 tablespoons chopped fresh parsley

1 teaspoon dried thyme

1 bay leaf

1 cup frozen green peas, thawed

1. Rinse chicken, pat dry with paper towels, and sprinkle chicken with salt and pepper. Heat oil in a large skillet over medium-high heat. Add chicken pieces to the pan, and brown well on all sides, turning gently with tongs, and being careful not to crowd the pan. Remove chicken from the pan, and set aside.

2. Add kielbasa, celery, onion, green pepper, and garlic to the pan, and cook, stirring frequently, for 3 minutes, or until onion is translucent. Add rice to the pan, and cook for 1 minute, stirring constantly. Add stock, parsley, thyme, and bay leaf to the pan, and bring to a boil over high heat, stirring frequently.

3. Return chicken to the pan, cover the pan, reduce the heat to medium-low, and cook for 25–35 minutes, or until chicken is cooked through and no longer pink, and almost all liquid has been absorbed.
4. Stir peas into the pan, recover the pan, and cook for 2–3 minutes, or until hot and remaining liquid is absorbed. Remove and discard bay leaf, season to taste with salt and pepper, and serve immediately.

Note: The dish can be cooked up to 2 days in advance and refrigerated, tightly covered. Reheat in a 350°F oven, covered, for 20–25 minutes, or until hot.

Variations: Like the Spanish paella on which it is based, this dish can succeed with any number of flavor combinations:
- Cut back on the amount of sausage, and add some 1-inch cubes of fish.
- For a spicier dish, substitute Cajun andouille sausage for the milder kielbasa.
- Place some well-scrubbed littleneck clams on top of the mixture for the last 10 minutes of baking, or until the clams open.

Turmeric is called "poor man's saffron"; it gives food the same vivid yellow color at a fraction of the cost. It is turmeric that colors commercial yellow rice, and you can use this spice any time saffron is specified in a recipe.

Chicken Cooked in Red Wine (Coq au Vin)

Everyone needs a good chicken in red wine recipe in their collection, if for no other reason than to serve a hearty red wine with a white meat on a cold winter night. I like this rendition since the smoky taste of the bacon emerges.

Yield: 4–6 servings | **Active time:** 20 minutes | **Start to finish:** 1¼ hours

> 1 (3½–4-pound) frying chicken, cut into serving pieces
> ¼ pound bacon, cut into 1-inch pieces
> Salt and freshly ground black pepper to taste
> ½ cup all-purpose flour
> 6 scallions, white parts and 3 inches of green tops, rinsed, trimmed, and sliced
> 1 pound small mushrooms, wiped with a damp paper towel and trimmed
> 2 garlic cloves, peeled and minced
> 12–18 small redskin potatoes, scrubbed and halved (quartered if larger than a walnut)
> 2 cups dry red wine
> 1 cup Chicken Stock (recipe on page 33) or purchased stock
> 2 tablespoons chopped fresh parsley
> 2 teaspoons dried thyme
> 2 bay leaves
> 1 (1-pound) package frozen pearl onions, thawed and drained

1. Preheat the oven to 350°F. Rinse chicken and pat dry with paper towels.
2. Place a large Dutch oven or roasting pan over medium-high heat, and cook bacon for 5–7 minutes, or until crisp. Remove bacon from the pan with a slotted spoon, and set aside; discard all but 3 tablespoons bacon fat. Sprinkle chicken with salt and pepper, and dust chicken pieces with flour, shaking off any excess.

3. Add chicken pieces to the pan, and brown well on all sides over medium-high heat, turning gently with tongs, and being careful not to crowd the pan. Remove chicken from the pan, and add scallions, mushrooms, and garlic. Cook, stirring frequently, for 3 minutes, or until scallions are translucent.
4. Return chicken to the pan, along with reserved bacon, potatoes, wine, chicken stock, parsley, thyme, salt, pepper, and bay leaves. Bring to a boil on top of the stove, and then cover the pan and bake in the center of the oven for 45 minutes. Add onions, and bake an additional 15 minutes, or until potatoes are tender. Remove and discard bay leaves, season to taste with salt and pepper, and serve immediately.

Note: The dish can be made up to 2 days in advance and refrigerated, tightly covered. Reheat it over low heat or in a 350°F oven for 30 minutes, or until hot.

In the past few years many wineries have started packaging very respectable drinking wine in boxes; the wine is contained in a plastic bag inside the box. This is a great way to keeping "cooking wine" around because no oxygen—the foe of wine—touches the contents.

Mexican Chicken with Molé Sauce

Molé, pronounced *MOH-lay,* is an ancient Mexican spicy sauce that dates from the Aztec era. What adds to its richness is unsweetened chocolate, and it always includes some sort of nut or legume for thickening. Serve this chicken with rice to enjoy the sauce.

Yield: 4–6 servings | **Active time:** 15 minutes | **Start to finish:** 55 minutes

1 (3½–4-pound) frying chicken, cut into serving pieces
5 tablespoons olive oil, divided
6 garlic cloves, peeled and minced, divided
4 tablespoons chili powder, divided
Salt and cayenne to taste
2 onions, peeled and chopped
2 teaspoons ground cumin
2 cups Chicken Stock (recipe on page 33) or purchased stock
1 (14.5-ounce) can diced tomatoes, drained
¼ cup peanut butter
¼ cup chopped raisins
1 tablespoon granulated sugar
1 tablespoon unsweetened cocoa powder

1. Preheat the oven to 350°F, and line a baking sheet with aluminum foil.
2. Rinse chicken and pat dry with paper towels. Combine 3 tablespoons oil, 2 garlic cloves, and 2 tablespoons chili powder in a small bowl. Season to taste with salt and cayenne. Mix well, and rub mixture on chicken. Arrange chicken on the prepared pan, skin side down.
3. Bake chicken for 20 minutes, then turn with tongs, and bake skin side up for an additional 20–25 minutes, or until chicken is cooked through and no longer pink, white meat registers 160°F and dark meat registers 165°F on an instant-read thermometer.
4. While chicken bakes, make sauce. Heat remaining 2 tablespoons oil in a heavy saucepan over medium-high heat. Add onions and remaining garlic and cook, stirring frequently, for 3 minutes, or until onions are translucent. Stir in remaining chili powder and cumin and cook, stirring constantly, for 1 minute.

5. Add chicken stock, tomatoes, peanut butter, raisins, sugar, and cocoa powder. Stir well, and bring to a boil over high heat. Reduce the heat to low and simmer sauce for 15 minutes, or until lightly thickened. Season to taste with salt and cayenne. Serve sauce on top of chicken.

Note: The sauce can be prepared up to 2 days in advance and refrigerated, tightly covered. Reheat over low heat, stirring occasionally.

Variations: This sauce can be used with a few other choices of protein:
- Pork chops can be substituted for the chicken pieces. Consult a similar recipe to determine the cooking time.
- Use the sauce to dress up hamburgers.

When cooking a dish such as this one, the most time-consuming part is making the sauce, so it makes great sense to double or even triple that part of the recipe. Freeze the majority of the sauce in heavy resealable plastic bags, and then this dish can be repeated with little effort in the future.

Old-Fashioned Chicken and Dumplings

Dumplings are biscuits that are steamed on the top of a simmering liquid, and they are a part of traditional colonial American cooking. Their addition on top of stewed chicken and vegetables makes this a one-dish meal.

Yield: 4–6 servings | **Active time:** 20 minutes | **Start to finish:** 1¼ hours

CHICKEN

1 (3½–4-pound) frying chicken, cut into serving pieces
Salt and freshly ground black pepper to taste
3 tablespoons vegetable oil
3 tablespoons unsalted butter
1 large onion, peeled and diced
2 carrots, peeled and sliced
2 celery ribs, rinsed, trimmed, and sliced
3 tablespoons all-purpose flour
3 cups Chicken Stock (recipe on page 33) or purchased stock
3 tablespoons chopped fresh parsley
2 teaspoons herbes de Provence
1 bay leaf
1 (10-ounce) package frozen peas, thawed

DUMPLINGS

1 cup all-purpose flour
1½ teaspoons baking powder
Pinch of salt
Pinch of freshly ground black pepper
1 tablespoon dried sage
3 tablespoons unsalted butter
⅓ cup milk

1. For chicken, rinse chicken, pat dry with paper towels, and sprinkle chicken with salt and pepper. Heat oil in a large skillet over medium-high heat. Add chicken pieces to the pan, and brown well on all sides, turning gently with tongs, and being careful not to crowd the pan. Remove chicken from the pan, and set aside. Discard fat from the pan.

2. Return the pan to the stove, and melt butter over medium heat. Add onion, carrots, and celery, and cook, stirring frequently, for 3 minutes, or until onion is translucent. Add flour, and cook for 2 minutes, stirring constantly. Add stock, parsley, herbes de Provence, and bay leaf to the pan, and bring to a boil.

3. Return chicken to the pan, cover the pan, and cook chicken over medium-low heat for 20–30 minutes, or until chicken is cooked through and no longer pink.

4. While chicken simmers, prepare dumpling dough. Combine flour, baking powder, salt, pepper, and sage in a mixing bowl. Cut in butter using a pastry blender, two knives, or your fingertips until mixture resembles coarse crumbs. Add milk, and stir to blend. Knead dough lightly on lightly floured counter, then cut into 12 parts and make each part into a patty.

5. Add peas to chicken mixture, remove and discard bay leaf, and place dough rounds on top of chicken. Cover the pan and cook for 15 minutes, or until dumplings are puffed and cooked through. Do not uncover the pan while dumplings steam. Serve immediately.

Note: The chicken mixture can be cooked up to 1 day in advance and refrigerated, tightly covered. Reheat it over medium heat to a simmer, stirring occasionally, before completing recipe. Do not make dumpling dough until just prior to serving.

Baking powder does not live forever, and if you don't do very much baking it's a good idea to test the potency before using it. Stir a few teaspoons into a glass of cold water. It should fizz furiously. If not, buy a new box.

Mexican Chicken and Rice (Arroz con Pollo)

This is one of those wonderful all-in-one dishes; the rice cooks in the same savory Mexican sauce as the pieces of chicken. It's incredibly flavorful, without being overly spicy.

Yield: 4–6 servings | **Active time:** 20 minutes | **Start to finish:** 50 minutes

1 (3½–4-pound) frying chicken, cut into serving pieces, with each
   breast half cut in half
Salt and freshly ground black pepper to taste
3 tablespoons olive oil
1 large onion, peeled and diced
3 garlic cloves, peeled and minced
1 cup long-grain white rice
1 (14.5-ounce) can diced tomatoes, drained
1 (4-ounce) can diced mild green chiles, drained
1 ¾ cups Chicken Stock (recipe on page 33) or purchased stock
1 tablespoon ground cumin
2 teaspoons dried oregano
1 bay leaf
½ cup sliced pimiento-stuffed green olives
1 (10-ounce) package frozen peas, thawed

1. Rinse chicken, pat dry with paper towels, and sprinkle chicken with salt and pepper. Heat oil in a large skillet over medium-high heat. Add chicken pieces to the pan, and brown well on all sides, turning gently with tongs, and being careful not to crowd the pan. Remove chicken from the pan, and set aside.
2. Add onion and garlic to the pan, and cook, stirring frequently, for 3 minutes, or until onion is translucent. Add rice to the pan, and cook for 1 minute, stirring constantly. Add tomatoes, green chiles, stock, cumin, oregano, and bay leaf to the pan, and bring to a boil over high heat, stirring frequently.
3. Return chicken to the pan, cover the pan, reduce the heat to medium-low, and cook for 25–35 minutes, or until chicken is tender and no longer pink, and almost all liquid has been absorbed.

4. Stir olives and peas into the pan, cover the pan again, and cook for 2–3 minutes, or until hot and remaining liquid is absorbed. Remove and discard bay leaf, season to taste with salt and pepper, and serve immediately.

Note: The dish can be cooked up to 2 days in advance and refrigerated, tightly covered. Reheat in a 350°F oven, covered, for 20–25 minutes, or until hot.

There are two types of small cans of chiles in the Hispanic food section of supermarkets. What is specified here are the mild green chiles, but the small cans of fiery jalapeño peppers look very similar. Look at the cans carefully; not only would jalapeño peppers waste your money, they would ruin this dish.

Chicken Cacciatore

Cacciatore is Italian for "hunter's style." A number of dishes from chicken to beef to veal use cacciatore as a handle, but all it means is that the dish is cooked with tomatoes and frequently wild mushrooms, too. The rest of the ingredients are up to the cook. Serve this over pasta or with polenta, and a tossed salad.

Yield: 4–6 servings | **Active time:** 20 minutes | **Start to finish:** 50 minutes

½ ounce dried porcini mushrooms
1 cup boiling Chicken Stock (recipe on page 33) or purchased stock
1 (3 ½–4-pound) frying chicken, cut into serving pieces
Salt and freshly ground black pepper to taste
¼ cup olive oil
¼ pound Genoa salami, finely chopped
1 large onion, peeled and chopped
4 garlic cloves, peeled and minced
½ pound white mushrooms, wiped with a damp paper towel, stems trimmed, and sliced
1 (28-ounce) can diced tomatoes, undrained
3 tablespoons chopped fresh parsley
1 teaspoon Italian seasoning
1 bay leaf

1. Soak dried porcini in boiling stock for 10 minutes. Drain, reserving soaking liquid. Discard stems and finely chop mushrooms, and strain liquid through paper coffee filter or paper towel. Reserve mushrooms and liquid.
2. Rinse chicken, pat dry with paper towels, and sprinkle chicken with salt and pepper. Heat oil in a large skillet over medium-high heat. Add chicken pieces to the pan, and brown well on all sides, turning gently with tongs, and being careful not to crowd the pan. Remove chicken from the pan, and set aside.
3. Add salami, onion, and garlic to the pan. Cook, stirring frequently, for 3 minutes, or until onion is translucent. Add white mushrooms, and cook for 2 minutes, stirring frequently.

4. Return chicken to the pan, and add chopped porcini, reserved stock, tomatoes, parsley, Italian seasoning, and bay leaf. Bring to a boil, and cook over low heat, covered, 25–35 minutes, or until chicken is cooked through and no longer pink. Remove and discard bay leaf, season to taste with salt and pepper, and serve immediately.

Note: The dish can be cooked up to 2 days in advance and refrigerated, tightly covered. Reheat in a 350°F oven, covered, for 20–25 minutes, or until hot.

Many Italian dishes are written to use prosciutto as a seasoning and flavoring agent, but prosciutto—even domestic prosciutto—falls into the category of luxury foods. I've discovered that salami serves the same purpose at a much lower cost.

Italian Stuffed Chicken Thighs

Part of the elegance of Italian cooking is its simplicity, and this chicken dish embodies that principle. The herbed cheese and salami stuffing moistens and flavors the chicken, so no sauce is necessary. I serve these thighs with lightly sauced pasta and a tossed salad.

Yield: 4–6 servings | **Active time:** 20 minutes | **Start to finish:** 45 minutes

> 8–12 chicken thighs, with skin and bones
> 2 ounces chopped Genoa salami
> 1 cup grated whole-milk mozzarella cheese
> 1 tablespoon dried sage
> 2 tablespoons olive oil
> 1 tablespoon Italian seasoning
> Salt and freshly ground black pepper to taste

1. Preheat the oven to 375°F, and line a baking sheet with aluminum foil. Rinse chicken and pat dry with paper towels.
2. Combine salami, cheese, and sage in a mixing bowl. Stuff mixture under skin of each chicken piece, and secure thighs closed with toothpicks.
3. Rub thighs with olive oil, and sprinkle with Italian seasoning, salt, and pepper. Arrange chicken on baking sheet, skin side down.
4. Bake chicken for 20 minutes, then turn with tongs, and bake skin side up for an additional 20–25 minutes, or until chicken is cooked through and no longer pink, and registers 165°F on an instant-read thermometer.

Note: The thighs can be stuffed up to 3 hours in advance and refrigerated, tightly covered with plastic wrap.

Variations: This stuffing is a wonderful addition to many meats:
- Cut a pocket in pork chops and fill it with the stuffing.
- Use it to stuff a flank steak.

Chicken with Garlic and Lemon

This easy recipe is my rendition of the French "chicken with 40 cloves of garlic." I actually use even more, and the sweet nuttiness of the garlic is contrasted with the tangy lemon juice. And both are terrific with chicken. Serve this with rice, and you can eat the cloves in their skin, or pop them out.

Yield: 4–6 servings | **Active time:** 10 minutes | **Start to finish:** 10 minutes

1 (3½–4-pound) frying chicken, cut into serving pieces
¼ cup olive oil
3 heads garlic, separated into cloves but not peeled
½ cup lemon juice
2 cups Chicken Stock (recipe on page 33) or purchased stock
Salt and freshly ground black pepper to taste
2 teaspoons cornstarch
2 tablespoons cold water

1. Preheat the oven to 400°F. Rinse chicken pieces, and pat dry with paper towels. Heat olive oil in a large ovenproof skillet over medium-high heat. Add chicken pieces and garlic cloves, and brown well, turning pieces with tongs.
2. Place chicken pieces skin side down, and pour lemon juice and stock into the pan. Bake chicken for 20 minutes, then turn with tongs, and bake skin side up for an additional 20–25 minutes, or until chicken is cooked through and no longer pink, and white meat registers 160°F and dark meat registers 165°F on an instant-read thermometer.
3. Place chicken pieces on a serving platter, and scatter garlic cloves around them. Cover chicken loosely with foil.
4. Bring sauce back to a boil on the stove and reduce by ¼. Combine cornstarch and water in a small bowl, and add to sauce. Simmer 1 minute, or until slightly thickened. Serve immediately.

Note: The dish can be made up to 2 days in advance and refrigerated, tightly covered. Reheat it, covered, in a 350°F oven for 30 minutes, or until hot.

Variation: If you're a garlic fan, try this:
- Substitute bone-in pork chops for the chicken, and cook them for a total of 30 minutes.

Grilled Chicken Thighs with Yogurt Mint Sauce

While many Americans think of mint in the context of heady juleps, or a sweet jelly to serve with lamb, in both Middle Eastern and Indian cooking it is a versatile culinary herb. These thighs are marinated in a yogurt base that tenderizes them, and then topped with a minty-fresh sauce.

Yield: 4–6 servings | **Active time:** 20 minutes | **Start to finish:** 3¾ hours, including 3 hours for marinating

> 8–12 boneless, skinless chicken thighs
> 1½ cups plain yogurt, divided
> ½ cup lemon juice
> 3 garlic cloves, peeled and minced, divided
> 1 tablespoon ground coriander
> 1 teaspoon dried thyme
> Salt and freshly ground black pepper to taste
> 2 tablespoons chopped fresh parsley
> 1 tablespoon chopped fresh mint
> 2 tablespoons olive oil
> 1 small red onion, peeled and thinly sliced
> 1 large tomato, rinsed, cored, seeded, and chopped

1. Rinse chicken and pat dry with paper towels. Prick chicken all over with a meat fork.

2. Combine 1 cup yogurt, lemon juice, 2 garlic cloves, coriander, thyme, salt, and pepper in a heavy resealable plastic bag. Mix well. Add chicken and marinate, refrigerated, for at least 3 hours or up to 24 hours, turning the bag occasionally.

3. While chicken marinates, prepare sauce. Combine remaining ½ cup yogurt, 1 garlic clove, parsley, mint, salt, and pepper in a mixing bowl, and whisk well. Refrigerate sauce until ready to serve, tightly covered.

4. Prepare a medium-hot gas or charcoal grill, or preheat the oven broiler.

5. Heat olive oil in a small skillet over medium-high heat. Add onion and cook, stirring frequently, for 3–5 minutes, or until onion is translucent. Add tomato, and cook for 3 minutes, stirring occasionally. Season mixture to taste with salt and pepper, and set aside.

6. Remove chicken from marinade, and discard marinade. Grill chicken for 10–12 minutes per side, or until cooked through and no longer pink and registers 165°F on an instant read thermometer. To serve, place chicken on each plate and top with some of onion mixture; pass sauce separately.

Note: Both the sauce and the onion mixture can be prepared up to 6 hours in advance. Refrigerate sauce and keep onion mixture at room temperature.

Turkey Chili

Making traditional chili with lean and inexpensive ground turkey has become more common in the past few years, and I adore it. The addition of a bit of cocoa powder adds a depth of flavor to the dish.

Yield: 6–8 servings | **Active time:** 15 minutes | **Start to finish:** 45 minutes

2 tablespoons olive oil
1 large onion, peeled and diced
3 garlic cloves, peeled and minced
1 large green bell pepper, seeds and ribs removed, and chopped
1½ pounds ground turkey
2 tablespoons all-purpose flour
3 tablespoons chili powder
2 tablespoons ground cumin
2 teaspoons dried oregano
2 teaspoons unsweetened cocoa powder
1 (28-ounce) can diced tomatoes, undrained
2 (15-ounce) cans kidney beans, drained and rinsed
Salt and cayenne to taste

1. Heat oil in a saucepan over medium-high heat. Add onion, garlic, and bell pepper. Cook, stirring frequently, for 3 minutes, or until onion is translucent. Add turkey and cook, stirring constantly, for 5 minutes, breaking up lumps with a fork.
2. Stir in flour, chili powder, cumin, oregano, and cocoa. Cook over low heat, stirring frequently, for 2 minutes. Add tomatoes and bring to a boil over medium heat. Simmer chili, partially covered and stirring occasionally, for 25 minutes, or until thick. Add beans, and cook for an additional 5 minutes. Season to taste with salt and cayenne.

Note: The dish can be prepared up to 2 days in advance and refrigerated, tightly covered. Reheat it, covered, in a saucepan over low heat.

Variations: Here are some ways to adapt this recipe:
- Substitute ground beef or ground pork for the turkey.
- There's a related dish in Mexican cooking called *picadillo*. Omit the oregano, and add ½ teaspoon ground cinnamon, ½ cup raisins, and 1 tablespoon cider vinegar to the chili.

Any chili can become a finger food by turning it into nachos. Pile the chili on large nacho corn chips, top with some grated Monterey Jack cheese, and pop under the broiler until the cheese is melted.

Turkey Meatball Hungarian Goulash

Goulash is the native stew of Hungary, and almost all meats end up cooked this flavorful way. Serve this dish over some buttered egg noodles with a steamed green vegetable for a contrasting color and flavor.

Yield: 4–6 servings | **Active time:** 25 minutes | **Start to finish:** 45 minutes

Vegetable oil spray
2 tablespoons olive oil
2 large onions, peeled and chopped
3 garlic cloves, peeled and minced
1 large egg
2 tablespoons whole milk
2 slices seeded rye bread
1¼ pounds ground turkey
Salt and freshly ground black pepper to taste
5 tablespoons paprika, preferably Hungarian
2 tablespoons tomato paste
2 cups Chicken Stock (recipe on page 33) or purchased stock
¾ cup sour cream

1. Preheat the oven broiler, line a rimmed baking sheet with heavy duty aluminum foil, and spray the foil with vegetable oil spray.
2. Heat oil in a small skillet over medium-high heat. Add onions and garlic and cook, stirring frequently, for 3 minutes, or until onion is translucent. While vegetables cook, combine egg and milk in a mixing bowl, and whisk until smooth. Break bread into tiny pieces and add to mixing bowl, and mix well.
3. Add ½ of onion mixture and turkey, season to taste with salt and pepper, and mix well again. Make mixture into 2-inch meatballs, and arrange meatballs on the prepared pan. Spray tops of meatballs with vegetable oil spray.
4. Broil meatballs 6 inches from the broiler element, turning them with tongs to brown all sides. While meatballs brown, add paprika to the skillet containing remaining onions and garlic. Cook over low heat for 1 minute, stirring constantly. Add tomato paste and stock and whisk well. Bring to a boil over medium-high heat, stirring occasionally.

5. Remove meatballs from the baking pan with a slotted spoon, and add meatballs to sauce. Bring to a boil, and simmer the meatballs, covered, over low heat, turning occasionally with a slotted spoon, for 15 minutes. Stir in sour cream, and serve immediately. *Do not allow sauce to boil.*

Note: The meatball mixture can be prepared up to 1 day in advance and refrigerated, tightly covered. Also, the dish can be cooked up to 2 days in advance and refrigerated, tightly covered. Reheat in a 350°F oven, covered, for 15–20 minutes, or until hot.

Variation: As a national dish, many foods are treated with the same sauce:

- Make the meatballs from ground pork or ground beef chuck.

Paprika is a seasoning used in many cuisines; the powder is made by grinding aromatic sweet red pepper pods several times. The color can vary from deep red to bright orange, and the flavor ranges from mild to pungent and hot.

Spicy Mexican Turkey-Zucchini Meatballs

Delicately flavored zucchini is the healthful surprise addition to these lean meatballs in a tomato sauce enlivened with spicy chipotle chiles. Serve this dish with rice or a small pasta.

Yield: 4–6 servings | **Active time:** 20 minutes | **Start to finish:** 45 minutes

> Vegetable oil spray
> 3 tablespoons olive oil
> 1 medium onion, peeled and chopped
> 1 small zucchini, rinsed, trimmed, and finely chopped
> 3 garlic cloves, peeled and minced
> 1 large egg
> 2 tablespoons whole milk
> ½ cup plain breadcrumbs
> 1 tablespoon dried oregano
> 1 teaspoon ground cumin
> 1¼ pounds ground turkey
> Salt and freshly ground black pepper to taste
> 1 (28-ounce) can crushed tomatoes in tomato puree
> 1–2 chipotle chiles in adobo sauce, drained

1. Preheat the oven broiler, line a rimmed baking sheet with heavy duty aluminum foil, and spray the foil with vegetable oil spray.

2. Heat oil in a skillet over medium-high heat. Add onion, zucchini, and garlic, and cook, stirring frequently, for 3 minutes, or until onion is translucent. While vegetables cook, combine egg and milk in a mixing bowl, and whisk until smooth. Add breadcrumbs, oregano, and cumin, and mix well.

3. Add onion mixture and turkey, season to taste with salt and pepper, and mix well again. Make mixture into 2-inch meatballs, and arrange meatballs on the prepared pan. Spray tops of meatballs with vegetable oil spray.

4. Broil meatballs 6 inches from the broiler element, turning them with tongs to brown all sides. While meatballs brown, combine ½ cup tomatoes and chiles in a blender or food processor fitted with a steel blade, and puree until smooth. Pour mixture into a saucepan with remaining tomatoes. Bring to a boil over medium-high heat, stirring occasionally.

5. Remove meatballs from the baking pan with a slotted spoon, and add meatballs to sauce. Bring to a boil, and simmer meatballs, covered, over low heat, turning occasionally with a slotted spoon, for 15 minutes. Serve immediately.

Note: The turkey mixture can be prepared up to 1 day in advance and refrigerated, tightly covered. Also, the dish can be cooked up to 2 days in advance and refrigerated, tightly covered. Reheat it in a 350°F oven, covered, for 15–20 minutes, or until hot.

Variation: Try this version too:
- Make the meatballs from a combination of ground chuck and chorizo sausage.

Zucchini is Italian in origin, and its native name was retained when it was integrated into American cooking. Choose small zucchini because they tend to have a sweeter flavor and the seeds are tender and less pronounced.

Sweet and Sour Chicken Meatballs

Most Americans were introduced to Chinese-American food with some sort of sweet and sour dish. There's rice right in these meatballs, so the meal is complete.

Yield: 4–6 servings | **Active time:** 25 minutes | **Start to finish:** 50 minutes

Vegetable oil spray

1¼ pounds ground chicken

1 cup cooked white rice

4 scallions, white parts and 3 inches of green tops, rinsed, trimmed, and chopped

4 garlic cloves, peeled and minced, divided

¼ cup soy sauce, divided

2 tablespoons Asian sesame oil*

Freshly ground black pepper to taste

¾ cup pineapple juice

½ cup ketchup

⅓ cup firmly packed light brown sugar

¼ cup cider vinegar

¼ cup water

1 tablespoon cornstarch

2 tablespoons vegetable oil

2 tablespoons grated fresh ginger

½ teaspoon crushed red pepper flakes, or to taste

1 sweet onion, such as Vidalia or Bermuda, peeled and sliced lengthwise

1 green or red bell pepper, seeds and ribs removed, and sliced

2 cups diced fresh pineapple

1. Preheat the oven to 450°F, line a rimmed baking sheet with heavy duty aluminum foil, and spray the foil with vegetable oil spray.

2. Combine chicken, rice, scallions, 2 garlic cloves, 2 tablespoons soy sauce, sesame oil, and pepper in a mixing bowl, and mix well. Make mixture into 1½-inch meatballs, and arrange meatballs on the prepared pan. Spray tops of meatballs with vegetable oil spray.

* Available in the Asian aisle of most supermarkets and in specialty markets.

3. Bake meatballs for 12–15 minutes, or until cooked through. Remove the pan from the oven, and set aside. Combine pineapple juice, ketchup, brown sugar, vinegar, water, and cornstarch in a bowl, and stir well to dissolve sugar. Set aside.
4. While meatballs bake, heat oil in a large skillet over high heat, swirling to coat. Add remaining garlic, ginger, and red pepper flakes, and stir-fry for 15 seconds, or until fragrant. Add onion and bell peppers and stir-fry for 1 minute. Add sauce and pineapple, and cook, stirring frequently, for 2 minutes, or until slightly thickened.
5. Remove meatballs from the baking pan with a slotted spoon, and add meatballs to the skillet. Cook 1 minute, and serve immediately.

Note: The chicken mixture can be prepared up to 1 day in advance and refrigerated, tightly covered. Also, the dish can be cooked up to 2 days in advance and refrigerated, tightly covered. Reheat it in a 350°F oven, covered, for 15–20 minutes, or until hot.

Variations: As is the case with many dishes on Chinese-American restaurant menus, this one can be changed to suit your taste in protein:
- Make the meatballs from beef, pork, or veal.
- Instead of pineapple, try mango or papaya as the fruit.

Basic Roast Chicken

There are few foods as wonderful as a perfectly roasted chicken, filling the house with aromas, and exiting the oven with crisp skin as dark as a Caribbean suntan. While a roasting chicken can feed a crowd, make a few at a time so that you'll have cooked chicken with which to feed the family later in the week.

Yield: 6–8 servings | **Active time:** 15 minutes | **Start to finish:** 2 hours

1 (5–7-pound) roasting chicken
4 sprigs fresh parsley, divided
4 sprigs fresh rosemary, divided
6 garlic cloves, peeled, divided
2 sprigs fresh thyme
Salt and freshly ground black pepper to taste
4 tablespoons (½ stick) unsalted butter, softened
1 large onion, peeled and roughly chopped
1 carrot, peeled and thickly sliced
1 celery rib, rinsed, trimmed, and sliced
1 cup Chicken Stock (recipe on page 33) or purchased stock

1. Preheat the oven to 425°F. Rinse chicken, and pat dry with paper towels. Place 2 sprigs parsley, 2 sprigs rosemary, 4 garlic cloves, and thyme in cavity of chicken. Sprinkle salt and pepper inside cavity, and close it with skewers and string.

2. Chop remaining parsley, rosemary, and garlic. Mix with butter, and season to taste with salt and pepper. Gently stuff mixture under the skin of breast meat. Rub skin with salt and pepper. Place chicken on a rack in a roasting pan, breast side up.

3. Bake for 30 minutes, reduce the oven temperature to 350°F, and add onion, carrot, and celery to the roasting pan. Cook an additional 1–1½ hours, or until chicken is cooked through and no longer pink, and white meat registers 160°F and dark meat registers 165°F on an instant-read thermometer. Remove chicken from the oven, and allow it to rest on a heated platter for 10 minutes.

4. Spoon grease out of the pan, and add chicken stock. Stir over medium-high heat until liquid is reduced to a syrupy consistency. Strain sauce into a sauce boat, and add to it any liquid that accumulates on the platter when the chicken is carved. Serve immediately.

Note: The chicken can be roasted up to 3 hours in advance and kept at room temperature, covered with aluminum foil.

Variations: While the method remains the same, here are some other seasoning blends to flavor the chicken:

- Use 3 tablespoons smoked Spanish paprika, 1 tablespoon ground cumin, 1 tablespoon dried thyme, and 3 minced garlic cloves.
- Use 3 tablespoons Italian seasoning, 3 tablespoons chopped fresh parsley, and 3 garlic cloves.
- Use 3 tablespoons dried oregano and 5 garlic cloves, and add 1 sliced lemon to the cavity.
- Rather than chicken stock, deglaze the pan with white wine.

Here's how to carve a roast chicken: To add a flourish to carving that also assures crisp skin for all, first "unwrap" the breast. Use a well-sharpened knife and fork. Carve and serve one side at a time. From neck, cut just through skin down middle of breast and around side. Hook fork on skin at tail and roll skin back to neck. Holding bird with fork, remove leg by severing hip joint. Separate drumstick from thigh and serve. Cut thin slices of breast at slight angle and add a small piece of rolled skin to each serving. Repeat all steps for other side. Remove wings last.

Old-Fashioned American Chicken Pot Pie

Many people have a negative reaction to chicken pot pie because of all those tasteless renditions inflicted on them from the freezer case. But a *real* chicken pot pie, filled with vegetables in a flavorful sauce beneath a flaky crust, is a work of art.

Yield: 4–6 servings | **Active time:** 20 minutes | **Start to finish:** 55 minutes

5 tablespoons unsalted butter, divided
1 medium onion, peeled and diced
½ pound mushrooms, wiped with a damp paper towel, trimmed, and sliced
1 cup Chicken Stock (recipe on page 33) or purchased stock
1 large carrot, peeled and thinly sliced
2 celery ribs, rinsed, trimmed, and thinly sliced
1 (10-ounce) russet potato, peeled and cut into ½-inch dice
2 tablespoons chopped fresh parsley
½ teaspoon dried thyme
1 bay leaf
1 cup frozen peas, thawed
3 tablespoons all-purpose flour
1 cup half-and-half
Salt and freshly ground black pepper to taste
3 cups cooked chicken, cut into ½-inch dice
½ ounces (½ of a 17-ounce package) puff pastry, thawed
1 large egg
1 tablespoon milk

1. Preheat the oven to 375°F, and grease a 9x13-inch baking pan.
2. Heat 2 tablespoons butter in a medium skillet over medium-high heat. Add onion and mushrooms, and cook, stirring frequently, for 5 minutes, or until mushrooms soften. Add stock, carrot, celery, potato, parsley, thyme, and bay leaf to skillet. Bring to a boil, reduce the heat to low, and simmer, uncovered, for 8–10 minutes, or until potato is tender. Add peas to pan, and cook 2 minutes. Strain mixture, reserving stock. Remove and discard bay leaf, and transfer vegetables to the prepared pan.

3. Heat remaining butter in a medium saucepan over low heat. Stir in flour, and cook for 2 minutes, stirring constantly. Whisk in reserved stock, and bring to a boil over medium-high heat, whisking constantly. Add half-and-half, and simmer 2 minutes. Season to taste with salt and pepper. Add chicken to the pan with vegetables, and stir in sauce.

4. Roll puff pastry into an 11x15-inch rectangle. Beat egg lightly with milk. Brush egg mixture around the outside edge of the pan. Place pastry on top of the pan, and crimp the edges, pressing to seal the pastry to the sides of the pan. Brush top of pastry with egg mixture, and cut in 6 (1-inch) vents to allow steam to escape.

5. Bake pie for 35 minutes, or until pastry is golden brown. Serve immediately.

Note: The filling can be made 1 day in advance and refrigerated, tightly wrapped. Reheat it in a microwave oven or in a saucepan over low heat, stirring frequently, before baking the pie.

The purpose of an egg wash is to give pastry a browned and shiny crust. But it's important to brush the crust before cutting the steam vents. The egg wash can clog the vents, which will create a soggy crust.

Chicken and Cheese Enchiladas

Enchiladas are a Mexican specialty, and the only constants are that they are a hot dish made with corn tortillas, and they contain some sort of cheese. They can be vegetarian or contain poultry, meat, or seafood.

Yield: 6–8 servings | **Active time:** 20 minutes | **Start to finish:** 50 minutes

2 tablespoons olive oil

1 large onion, peeled and chopped

3 garlic cloves, peeled and minced

1 jalapeño or serrano chile, seeds and ribs removed, and finely chopped

2 tablespoons chili powder

1 tablespoons ground cumin

1 teaspoon dried oregano

1 (4-ounce) can diced mild green chiles, drained

3 cups shredded cooked chicken

1 (3-ounce) package cream cheese, softened

2 cups grated Monterey Jack cheese, divided

Salt and freshly ground black pepper to taste

3 tablespoons unsalted butter

3 tablespoons all-purpose flour

1 cup Chicken Stock (recipe on page 33) or purchased stock

1 cup half-and-half

12–16 (6-inch) corn tortillas

Vegetable oil spray

1. Preheat the oven to 400°F, and grease a 10x14-inch baking pan.
2. Heat oil in a small skillet over medium-high heat. Add onion, garlic, and chile. Cook, stirring frequently, for 3 minutes, or until onion is translucent. Add chili powder, cumin, and oregano. Cook, stirring constantly, for 1 minute. Add canned chiles, and set aside.
3. Combine chicken, cream cheese, and 1 cup Monterey Jack cheese in a mixing bowl. Season to taste with salt and pepper, and set aside.

4. Heat butter in a saucepan over low heat. Stir in flour, and cook, stirring constantly, for 2 minutes. Whisk in stock, and bring to a boil over medium-high heat, whisking constantly. Add half-and-half, and simmer 2 minutes. Stir in cooked vegetables, and season to taste with salt and pepper.

5. Heat a large non-stick skillet over medium heat. Spray tortillas lightly with vegetable oil spray, and cook for 10 seconds per side, turning gently with tongs. Tortillas should be pliable, but not crisp.

6. Place 1/3 of sauce in the bottom of the prepared pan. Divide chicken mixture into tortillas, and roll each gently. Arrange enchiladas seam side down in the pan. Pour remaining sauce over top, and cover pan with aluminum foil. Bake for 10 minutes, uncover pan, sprinkle with remaining cheese, and bake for 15–20 minutes, or until bubbly and browned. Allow to sit for 5 minutes before serving.

Note: The dish can be prepared up to baking 1 day in advance and refrigerated, tightly covered. Add 10 minutes to covered bake time if filling is chilled.

Chicken Croquettes

Croquettes of all types have been used as a way to stretch leftovers for centuries; they are basically a thick white sauce into which cooked food is folded, formed into patties, and fried. I adore them, and they are very easy to make.

Yield: 4–6 servings | **Active time:** 20 minutes | **Start to finish:** 1½ hours, including 1 hour to chill mixture

4 tablespoons (½ stick) unsalted butter
1 small onion, peeled and finely chopped
1 cup all-purpose flour, divided
⅔ cup whole milk
⅔ cup Chicken Stock (recipe on page 33) or purchased stock
3 cups finely chopped cooked chicken
2 tablespoons chopped fresh parsley
1 tablespoon Cajun seasoning
2 large eggs, lightly beaten
2 tablespoons water
1 cup plain breadcrumbs
1 cup Basic White Sauce (recipe on page 30)
¾ cup grated Swiss cheese
Salt and freshly ground black pepper to taste
2 cups vegetable oil for frying

1. Heat butter in a saucepan over medium heat. Add onion and cook, stirring frequently, for 2 minutes. Add ⅓ cup flour, reduce the heat to low, and cook for 2 minutes, stirring constantly. Whisk in milk and stock, and bring to a boil over medium heat, whisking constantly. Reduce the heat to low, and simmer sauce for 2 minutes. Remove the pan from the heat.

2. Stir chicken, parsley, and Cajun seasoning into sauce, and transfer mixture to a 9x13-inch baking pan. Spread mixture evenly, and refrigerate for 30 minutes, or until cold, loosely covered with plastic wrap.

3. Place remaining flour on a sheet of plastic wrap, combine egg and water in a shallow bowl, and place breadcrumbs on another sheet of plastic wrap. With wet hands, form chilled chicken mixture into 2-inch balls, and flatten balls into patties. Dust patties with flour, dip into egg mixture, and dip into breadcrumbs, pressing to ensure crumbs adhere. Refrigerate patties for 30 minutes.
4. While patties chill, make Basic White Sauce. Add cheese, and stir until cheese melts. Season to taste with salt and pepper, and keep warm.
5. Heat oil in a deep-sided skillet over medium-high heat to 375°F. Add patties, being careful not to crowd the pan. Cook for a total of 3–5 minutes, or until browned. Remove croquettes from the pan with a slotted spoon, and drain well on paper towels. Serve immediately, passing sauce separately.

Note: The croquettes can be prepared for frying up to 1 day in advance and refrigerated, tightly covered. They can also be fried in advance; reheat them in a 375°F oven for 10–12 minutes, or until hot and crusty again.

Variations: This recipe is a way to use up and stretch many types of cooked meat and seafood you might have around:
- Make them with turkey and follow this recipe.
- Make them with chopped ham, omitting the Cajun seasoning and adding 1 teaspoon dried sage, salt, and pepper.
- Make them with chopped fish or seafood—salmon, cod, halibut, shrimp, and crab all work well—and omit the Cajun seasoning and add 1 tablespoon Old Bay seasoning.

Chicken Hash

This is a great dish for brunch with fruit salad as well as at supper with a tossed salad. If you served a roast chicken with mashed potatoes, you can use them up, too, and save time as well as money.

Yield: 4–6 servings | **Active time:** 20 minutes | **Start to finish:** 1 hour

4 tablespoons (½ stick) unsalted butter
2 tablespoons olive oil
2 large sweet onions, such as Vidalia or Bermuda, peeled and diced
2 garlic cloves, peeled and minced
1 teaspoon granulated sugar
Salt and freshly ground black pepper to taste
1½ pounds redskin potatoes, scrubbed and cut into 1-inch dice
3 cups diced cooked chicken

1. Heat butter and olive oil in a large skillet over low heat. Add the onions and garlic, toss to coat, and cover the pan. Cook over low heat for 10 minutes, stirring occasionally. Uncover the pan, raise the heat to medium-high, sprinkle with sugar, salt, and pepper. Cook for 20–30 minutes, stirring frequently, until onions are brown. If onions stick to the pan, stir to incorporate browned juices.
2. Preheat the oven to 450°F, and grease a 9x13-inch baking pan.
3. While onions cook, place potatoes in a saucepan and cover with salted cold water. Bring potatoes to a boil over high heat, and boil for 10–12 minutes, or until potatoes are very tender when tested with a knife. Drain potatoes and mash them roughly with a potato masher. Add chicken and onions to potatoes, and mix well. Season to taste with salt and pepper.
4. Spread hash into the prepared pan, and bake for 15 minutes, or until top is lightly brown. Serve immediately.

Note: The hash can be prepared 2 days in advance and refrigerated, tightly covered. Reheat it, covered with aluminum foil, for 10 minutes, then remove the foil and bake for 15 minutes more.

When onions caramelize and turn brown the reaction is caused by the natural sugars in the vegetable. Adding a bit of granulated sugar speeds up the process.

Gazpacho Turkey Salad

No, this isn't a mistake; I know that gazpacho is a Spanish vegetable soup. But all the ingredients are in this refreshing salad, which is napped with a dressing similar to the other flavors in the soup.

Yield: 4–6 servings | **Active time:** 15 minutes | **Start to finish:** 25 minutes

1 pound cooked turkey, cut into ½-inch dice

1 green bell pepper, seeds and ribs removed, and cut into ½-inch dice

2 cucumbers, rinsed, seeded, and cut into ½-inch dice

1 small red onion, peeled and cut into ½-inch dice

3 large ripe tomatoes, rinsed, cored, seeded, and cut into ½-inch dice

⅓ cup chopped fresh cilantro

1 jalapeño or serrano chile, seeds and ribs removed, and finely chopped

3 garlic cloves, peeled and minced

¼ cup balsamic vinegar

Salt and freshly ground black pepper to taste

⅓ cup olive oil

4–6 cups chopped iceberg or romaine lettuce

1. Combine turkey, green pepper, cucumbers, red onion, and tomatoes in a large mixing bowl.
2. Combine cilantro, chile, garlic, vinegar, salt, and pepper in a jar with a tight-fitting lid. Shake well, add olive oil, and shake well again. Pour dressing over salad, and refrigerate 10 minutes.
3. Arrange lettuce on individual plates or a serving platter and mound salad in the center. Serve immediately.

Note: The salad can be prepared 4 hours in advance and refrigerated, tightly covered. Do not add dressing until 10 minutes before serving.

Variations: What makes this salad is the combination of vegetables and the flavors in the dressing. Here are other options:
- Substitute cooked fish for the turkey.
- Substitute cubed and sautéed zucchini or yellow squash for the turkey.

Turkey Tetrazzini

This grandmother of all leftover poultry casseroles was named for Italian singer Luisa Tetrazzini, who was the toast of the American opera circuit in the early 1900s. Where the dish was created, and by whom, is not known.

Yield: 6–8 servings | **Active time:** 20 minutes | **Start to finish:** 50 minutes

1 pound thin spaghetti, broken into 2-inch lengths
4 tablespoons (½ stick) unsalted butter, divided
2 tablespoons olive oil
1 small onion, peeled and chopped
2 garlic cloves, peeled and minced
2 celery ribs, rinsed, trimmed, and thinly sliced
½ pound mushrooms, wiped with a damp paper towel, trimmed, and sliced
3 tablespoons all-purpose flour
½ cup dry sherry
1 cup Chicken Stock (recipe on page 33) or purchased stock
1½ cups half-and-half
3 cups shredded cooked turkey
1 cup freshly grated Parmesan cheese, divided
Salt and freshly ground black pepper to taste
½ cup breadcrumbs

1. Preheat the oven to 350°F, and grease a 10x14-inch baking pan. Bring a large pot of salted water to a boil, and cook pasta according to package directions until al dente. Drain, and place pasta in the prepared pan.

2. Heat 2 tablespoons butter and olive oil in a large skillet over medium-high heat. Add onion, garlic, and celery, and cook, stirring frequently, for 3 minutes, or until onion is translucent. Add mushrooms, and cook for 3 minutes, or until mushrooms soften. Add vegetables to the pan with pasta.

3. Heat remaining butter in saucepan over low heat. Stir in flour and cook, stirring constantly, for 2 minutes. Whisk in sherry, and bring to a boil over medium-high heat, whisking constantly. Simmer 3 minutes, then add stock and half-and-half, and simmer 2 minutes.
4. Stir turkey and ¾ cup Parmesan cheese into sauce, and season to taste with salt and pepper. Combine mixture with pasta and vegetables in the prepared pan. Cover pan with aluminum foil, and bake for 15 minutes. Combine remaining Parmesan cheese with breadcrumbs. Uncover the pan, sprinkle breadcrumb mixture on top, and bake an additional 15–20 minutes, or until bubbly and top is browned. Serve immediately.

Note: The dish can be prepared up to baking 1 day in advance and refrigerated, tightly covered. Add 10 minutes to covered bake time if filling is chilled.

Mexican Turkey "Lasagna"

Corn tortillas are used in place of pasta to separate the layers of this dish, which contains ricotta, as well as cooked turkey, in a lively tomato sauce.

Yield: 6–8 servings | **Active time:** 15 minutes | **Start to finish:** 50 minutes

3 tablespoons olive oil

1 large onion, peeled and diced

2 garlic cloves, peeled and minced

1 tablespoon chili powder

1 teaspoon ground cumin

1 teaspoon dried oregano

1 (14.5-ounce) can diced tomatoes, drained

1 (8-ounce) can tomato sauce

1 (15-ounce) can kidney beans, drained and rinsed

3 cups shredded cooked turkey

Salt and freshly ground black pepper to taste

1½ cups whole-milk ricotta cheese

2 large eggs, lightly beaten

1 (4-ounce) can diced mild green chiles, drained

3 tablespoons chopped fresh cilantro

12 (6-inch) corn tortillas

1½ cups grated Monterey Jack cheese, divided

1. Preheat the oven to 375°F, and grease a 9x13-inch baking pan.

2. Heat oil in a large skillet over medium-high heat. Add onion and garlic, and cook, stirring frequently, for 3 minutes, or until onion is translucent. Stir in chili powder, cumin, and oregano. Cook, stirring constantly, for 1 minute. Add tomatoes, tomato sauce, beans, and turkey. Bring to a boil, and simmer 2 minutes. Season to taste with salt and pepper, and set aside.

3. Combine ricotta, eggs, chiles, and cilantro in a mixing bowl. Season to taste with salt and pepper, and stir well.

4. Place ¹/₂ of turkey mixture in the bottom of the prepared pan. Top with 6 tortillas, overlapping them to cover filling. Spread cheese mixture on top, and sprinkle with ¹/₂ cup Monterey Jack cheese. Layer remaining tortillas, then spread remaining turkey mixture and sprinkle with remaining cheese.

5. Cover the pan with aluminum foil, and bake for 15 minutes. Uncover the pan, and bake for an additional 20 minutes, or until bubbly and cheese melts. Allow to sit for 5 minutes, then serve.

Note: The dish can be prepared up to baking 1 day in advance and refrigerated, tightly covered. Add 10 minutes to the covered bake time if filling is chilled.

Variations: Here are other ways to enjoy this dish:
- Make it a vegetarian dish by substituting 2 small zucchini, sliced and cooked until tender in 2 tablespoons olive oil, for the turkey.
- For a spicier dish, use jalapeño Jack cheese instead of Monterey Jack.

Moroccan Chicken Salad

Tangy dried currants and succulent dried apricots meld with traditional Moroccan spices and add textural interest to the light couscous base of this toothsome chicken salad. It's refreshing on a summer day.

Yield: 4–6 servings | **Active time:** 15 minutes | **Start to finish:** 45 minutes

SALAD

4 1/2 cups water
3 cups (2 boxes of 10-ounces) plain couscous
1/2 cup dried currants
1/2 cup chopped dried apricots
3 cups diced cooked chicken
1 (15-ounce) can garbanzo beans, drained and rinsed
1/2 cup chopped pitted Kalamata or other brine-cured olives
1 small red onion, peeled and diced
1/2 small fennel bulb, rinsed, trimmed, and diced

DRESSING

1/2 cup orange juice
2 tablespoons balsamic vinegar
1/4 cup chopped fresh cilantro
2 garlic cloves, peeled and minced
1 tablespoon ground cumin
Salt and freshly ground black pepper to taste
1/4 cup olive oil

1. For salad, bring water to a boil in a saucepan over high heat. Add couscous, currants, and apricots. Cover the pan, turn off the heat, and let couscous stand for 10 minutes. Fluff mixture with a fork, and transfer it to a mixing bowl. Chill well.

2. While couscous chills, make dressing. Combine orange juice, vinegar, cilantro, garlic, cumin, salt, and pepper in a jar with a tight-fitting lid. Shake well. Add olive oil, and shake well again. Set aside.
3. Add chicken, beans, olives, onion, and fennel to couscous. Pour dressing over salad, and toss well. Serve chilled.

Note: The salad can be prepared 1 day in advance and kept refrigerated, tightly covered. Do not add the dressing until just before serving.

Variations: Like many entree salads, this one is a great way to use up leftovers:
- Substitute diced cooked fish for the chicken.
- Omit the chicken entirely, add 1 extra can of garbanzo beans, and serve it as a vegetarian dish.
- While dried fruit is important to flavor the dish, substitute any that you have around for the currants and apricots.

Although balsamic vinegar is reasonably priced, it is still more expensive than cider vinegar. If you don't use balsamic vinegar very often, it is not worth the money to keep a bottle in your kitchen. You can always substitute cider vinegar.

Chapter 6:
"Meating" the Challenge

Welcome to the wonderful world of slowly cooked meats; that's what you'll find in this chapter. If you are going to splurge and grill a steak or some lamb chops, you probably already know how to do it, and the title of this book excludes them from consideration. I've yet to find a steak that is less than $3 a serving—unless the servings are Lilliputian. The same is true for veal, which is exorbitantly expensive because the animal is so young and small.

But that doesn't mean you can't revel in delicious beefy flavor when cooking the recipes in this chapter! You'll find sensational stews and succulent pot roast, and dishes made with ground beef and ground lamb drawn from cuisines around the world.

Pork and ham are also represented, because both meats continue to represent a substantial price-value relationship.

SLOWLY DOES IT

Most of the dishes in this chapter fall under the generic category of braised food. No cuisine can claim braising, although we've borrowed our English word from the French. Every culture has less tender cuts of meat, which are usually also less expensive, that are simmered in aromatic liquid for many hours until they're tender; that's what braising is all about—tenderness.

The process is referred to as braising when dealing with a large roast, and stewing when the meat is cut into small cubes. Stew also implies that vegetables are added somewhere along the way. Braising is a low heat method, since the meat is the same temperature as the simmering liquid, 212°F. This simmering converts the collagen of the meat's connective tissue to gelatin, so the meat becomes tender. There is no fear that the outside will be dried out, as in high heat dry roasting, both because the food is covered in the pan and because the pan contains liquid, which produces a moist heat.

This low temperature cooking method is also the reason that it takes almost as long to cook a stew, with meat in small pieces, as it does to braise a large roast. The only difference is the time the meat takes to reach the same temperature as the liquid. That's why you can substitute a large roast for cubes in any stew recipes, and vice versa.

CHOOSING YOUR CUTS

In the same way that cutting up your own chickens saves money, taking a large piece of beef and cutting into cubes for stew is economical. But unlike cutting up chickens, there is no exact science to "breaking down" a roast for stewing; just cut away all visible fat and discard the bones. Don't worry about the gristle; that will soften as the beef braises.

The general guideline is that if it's less expensive, then it's the cut you want, but here are some specifics:

- Chuck is the beef taken from between the neck and shoulder blades. Some chuck roasts also contain a piece of the blade bone, but it's easy to cut up a chuck roast, and it's the most flavorful cut.

- Round is the general name for the large quantity of beef from the hind leg extending from the rump to the ankle. The eye of the round and the bottom round are the two least tender cuts, while the top round should be reserved for roasting.

- Brisket is taken from the breast section under the first five ribs, and the leaner piece is called the flat cut while the fattier piece is the point cut. Brisket makes a succulent pot roast, but it's not recommended for cutting into cubes for stewing because the fibers are distinct and the meat can become stringy if cubed.

- Ground beef is made from the less tender and less popular cuts of beef, although it sometimes includes trimmings from more tender cuts like steak. The price of ground beef is determined by the cut of meat from which it was made and the amount of fat incorporated into the mix. High-fat mixtures are less costly but will shrink more when cooked. The least expensive product is sold as ground beef; it's made from the shank and brisket, and can contain up to 30 percent fat. Moderately priced ground chuck is the next level of ground beef. Because it contains enough fat (about 15–20 percent) to give it flavor and make it juicy, yet not enough to cause excess shrinkage, ground chuck is a good choice for these recipes. A few recipes in this chapter specify ground lamb. While once again made from the less tender cuts, there is no grading as there is for beef.

PROCEDURAL PROWESS

The one major principle for almost all the recipes in this chapter is the initial browning of the meat, which means cooking the meat quickly over moderately high heat. This causes the surface of the food to brown. In the case of cubes of beef for stew, browning seals in the juices and keeps the interior moist; for ground meats, browning gives food an appetizing color, allows you to drain off some of the inherent fat, and also gives dishes a rich flavor.

While larger pieces can be browned under an oven broiler, ground meats are browned in a skillet. Crumble the meat in a skillet over medium-high heat. Break up the lumps with a meat fork or the back of a spoon as it browns, and then stir it around frequently until all lumps are brown and no pink remains. At that point, it's easy to remove it from the pan with a slotted spoon, and discard the grease from the pan. You can then use the pan again without washing it for any pre-cooking of other ingredients.

CUTTING BACK ON FAT

In addition to cost, another benefit of braising meats is that it's possible to remove a great percentage of the saturated fat. It's easy to find and discard this "bad fat," both before and after cooking.

On raw meat, the fat is easy to spot. It's the white stuff around the red stuff. Cut it off with a sharp paring knife, and you're done. However, some fat remains in the tissue of the red meat, and much of this saturated fat is released during the cooking process. There are ways to discard it, when the food is either hot or cold.

If you're cooking in advance and refrigerating a dish, all the fat rises to the top and hardens once chilled. Just scrape it off, throw it away, and you're done. The same principle of fat rising to the surface is true when food is hot, but it's a bit harder to eliminate it. Tilt the pan, and the fat will form a puddle on the lower side. It's then easier to scoop it off with a soup ladle. When you're down to too little to scoop off, level the pan, and blot the top with paper towels.

PORCINE PLEASURES

Recent studies of randomly selected pork cuts from leading supermarkets in fifteen U.S. cities have shown that today's pork is 31 percent lower in fat, 17 percent lower in calories, and 10 percent lower in cholesterol than it was a few decades ago. In addition, more than 60 percent of the fat in pork is unsaturated. This compares favorably with beef and lamb, which are 52 percent and 44 percent unsaturated, respectively.

Agricultural professionals attribute the reduction of fat content in part to improvements in the breeding and feeding of pigs. Retailers are also trimming fat more closely from pork cuts, so people are getting more lean meat for their dollar.

COMPATIBLE ANIMALS AND CONVERTIBLE RECIPES

Often you can change the meat without sacrificing the quality of a recipe as long as the change is in the same flavor and texture family. For example, beef and lamb are interchangeable in recipes because both are hearty meats. The question you should ask yourself is: Is it a red meat or a white meat? Even though veal is a young cow, the flavor and texture is more similar to pork or chicken than it is to beef. But veal is too expensive to cook very often, so if you have a favorite veal recipe, try making it with pork.

Braised Beef with Rosemary and Celery

Aromatic rosemary and delicate celery transform this pot roast into a lighter and more elegant dish. Serve it with some buttered egg noodles or steamed potatoes, and a green vegetable.

Yield: 6–8 servings | **Active time:** 20 minutes | **Start to finish:** 3 hours

1 (3-pound) boneless chuck roast or brisket
Salt and freshly ground black pepper to taste
¼ cup all-purpose flour
3 tablespoons olive oil
3 large onions, peeled and diced
6 celery ribs, rinsed, trimmed, and sliced
4 garlic cloves, peeled and minced
2 ½ cups Beef Stock (recipe on page 34) or purchased stock
3 tablespoons chopped fresh rosemary or 1 tablespoon dried

1. Preheat the oven to 350°F. Rinse beef and pat dry with paper towels. Season with salt and pepper and rub with flour, shaking off excess over the sink or a garbage can.
2. Heat oil in a Dutch oven over medium-high heat. Add beef and cook, turning with tongs, until browned on all sides. Remove beef from the pan, and add onions, celery, and garlic. Cook, stirring frequently, for 3 minutes, or until onions are translucent.
3. Return beef to the pan, and add stock and rosemary. Bring to a boil on top of the stove, then transfer to the oven, and bake for 2–2½ hours, or until fork tender.
4. Remove beef to a warm platter and tip the Dutch oven to spoon off as much grease as possible. Cook sauce over medium heat until reduced by ½. Season sauce to taste with salt and pepper, then pour sauce over beef, and serve immediately.

Note: The beef can be prepared up to 3 days in advance and refrigerated. If cooked in advance, remove the layer of grease, which will have hardened on the top. Reheat, covered, in a 350°F oven for 25–35 minutes, or until hot.

Guinness Beef Stew

This is a heartier version of the classic Belgian dish, *Carbonnade Flemande,* which is beef cooked in a light beer. It's traditionally served with steamed potatoes, but I like roasted potatoes to provide some textural contrast.

Yield: 4–6 servings | **Active time:** 20 minutes | **Start to finish:** 3 hours

- 1 (2-pound) chuck roast, trimmed and cut into 1-inch cubes, or 1½ pounds stewing beef, rinsed and patted dry with paper towels
- 3 tablespoons vegetable oil
- 4 large onions, peeled and thinly sliced
- 2 garlic cloves, peeled and minced
- 2 teaspoons granulated sugar
- Salt and freshly ground black pepper to taste
- 1½ cups Beef Stock (recipe on page 34) or purchased stock
- 1 (12-ounce) bottle Guinness Stout beer
- 2 tablespoons firmly packed dark brown sugar
- 2 tablespoons chopped fresh parsley
- 1 teaspoon dried thyme
- 1 bay leaf
- 1 tablespoon cornstarch
- 1 tablespoon cold water

1. Preheat the oven broiler, and line a broiler pan with heavy duty aluminum foil. Arrange beef in a single layer on the foil, and broil for 3 minutes per side, or until beef is lightly browned.
2. Preheat the oven to 350°F. Heat oil in a Dutch oven over medium heat. Add onions and garlic, toss to coat with fat, and cook, covered, for 10 minutes. Uncover the pan, raise the heat to medium-high, and sprinkle onions with granulated sugar, salt, and pepper. Cook, stirring occasionally, for 10–12 minutes, or until onions are lightly browned.
3. Return beef to the pan, and stir in stock, beer, brown sugar, parsley, thyme, and bay leaf. Bring to a boil on top of the stove, stirring.
4. Cover the pan, and bake for 2–2½ hours, or until meat is tender. Spoon off as much fat as possible from surface. Combine cornstarch and water in a small cup, and stir into stew. Cook over low heat for 2 minutes, or until slightly thickened. Serve immediately.

Note: The dish can be made up to 2 days in advance and refrigerated, tightly covered. Reheat it over low heat or in a 350°F oven for 30 minutes or until hot.

Beef Stroganoff Stew

Beef Stroganoff was named for a nineteenth-century Russian diplomat, Count Paul Stroganoff; it became a hallmark of what Americans called "continental cuisine" in the mid-twentieth century. While the original Beef Stroganoff is a quickly sautéed dish, this long-simmered braise has the same flavors of sour cream and a rich tomato sauce.

Yield: 4–6 servings | **Active time:** 15 minutes | **Start to finish:** 3 hours

1 (2-pound) chuck roast, trimmed and cut into 1-inch cubes, or 1½ pounds stewing beef, rinsed and patted dry with paper towels
Salt and freshly ground black pepper to taste
½ cup all-purpose flour
3 tablespoons vegetable oil
2 tablespoons unsalted butter
2 large onions, peeled and diced
2 garlic cloves, peeled and minced
½ pound mushrooms, wiped with a damp paper towel, trimmed, and sliced
2 tablespoons paprika
2 cups Beef Stock (recipe on page 34) or purchased stock
3 tablespoons tomato paste
2 tablespoons chopped fresh parsley
1 tablespoon Dijon mustard
½ cup sour cream

1. Preheat the oven to 350°F. Season meat to taste with salt and pepper, and dust meat with flour, shaking off any excess into the sink or a garbage can. Heat oil in a Dutch oven over medium-high heat. Add beef, and cook, turning pieces with tongs, until brown on all sides. Remove meat from the pan with slotted spoon, and set aside.
2. Add butter to the pan. When butter melts, add onion and garlic, and cook, stirring frequently, for 3 minutes, or until onion is translucent. Add mushrooms, and cook for 2 minutes more. Add paprika to the pan, and cook for 1 minute, stirring constantly.

3. Add stock, tomato paste, parsley, and mustard to the pan. Stir well, return meat to the pan, and bring to a boil on top of the stove, stirring occasionally.

4. Cover the pan, and bake for 2–2½ hours, or until meat is tender. Spoon off as much fat as possible from surface. Stir in sour cream, and season to taste with salt and pepper. *Do not allow dish to boil.* Serve immediately.

Note: **The dish can be made up to 2 days in advance and refrigerated, tightly covered. Reheat it over low heat or in a 350°F oven for 30 minutes, or until hot.**

Variation: Try this adaptation if you like the flavor of the sauce:

- Make the dish with boneless, skinless chicken thighs, and reduce the cooking time to 1½–2 hours.

Sweet and Sour Stuffed Cabbage

Stuffed cabbage, which comes from traditional German and Eastern European cooking, was brought to this country in the nineteenth century. This is my favorite version because it includes sweet and succulent fruits—both dried and fresh.

Yield: 4–6 servings | **Active time:** 20 minutes | **Start to finish:** 2 hours

1 (2-pound) head green cabbage
1 pound ground chuck
1¼ cups cooked rice
1 small onion, peeled and grated
Salt and freshly ground black pepper to taste
2 Golden Delicious apples, peeled, cored, and cut into ½-inch dice
½ cup raisins
1 (15-ounce) can tomato sauce
¾ cup cider vinegar
¾ cup firmly packed dark brown sugar

1. Preheat the oven to 375°F, and grease a 10x14-inch baking pan. Bring a large pot of water to a boil. Remove and discard broken outer leaves of cabbage. Core cabbage by cutting around all 4 sides of core with a heavy, sharp knife. Discard core, and spear cabbage in the resulting hole with a heavy meat fork.

2. Hold cabbage in boiling water, and pull off leaves with tongs as they become pliable. Continue until you have 8–12 leaves separated. Remove cabbage from water, and shred 2 additional cups cabbage. Scatter shredded cabbage into the bottom of the pan. Set leaves aside.

3. Combine beef, rice, onion, salt, and pepper in mixing bowl, and mix well. Place 1 cabbage leaf in front of you, and scoop ⅓ cup meat mixture into large end. Fold sides over meat, and roll leaf towards stem end. Place rolls in the baking pan, stem side down, and repeat with remaining leaves and meat. Scatter apples and raisins over meat rolls. Combine tomato sauce, vinegar, and brown sugar in mixing bowl, and stir well. Pour mixture over cabbage rolls.

4. Cover pan with aluminum foil, and bake for 1¼ hours. Remove foil, and bake an additional 15 minutes, or until lightly browned. Serve immediately.

Note: The dish can be cooked up to 2 days in advance and refrigerated, tightly covered. Reheat, covered with foil, in a 350°F oven for 25–30 minutes, or until hot.

Variations: Here are some other ways to make this dish:
- Substitute ground turkey or ground pork for the beef.
- Make the dish vegetarian by using 1 pound finely diced zucchini instead of meat.

After the cabbage has been submerged in the boiling water, some of the inner core will be hot and blanched, and the central core will still be cold and crisp. Shred the cabbage from the exterior in, and save the portion that is still crisp for cole slaw.

Baked Pasta with Beef and Beans (*Pasta Fazool*)

While the names of Italian pasta shapes sound romantic, they are merely the translations of the words that describe the look of the pasta. Penne means quills or pens, while mostaccioli means small mustaches. Either one of these hearty shapes is perfect with this meat sauce complemented with beans.

Yield: 6–8 servings | **Active time:** 15 minutes | **Start to finish:** 45 minutes

1 pound mostaccioli or penne pasta

1 pound bulk hot or sweet Italian sausage, or link sausage with casings discarded

½ pound ground chuck

2 tablespoons olive oil

1 large onion, peeled and chopped

4 garlic cloves, peeled and minced

1 teaspoon dried oregano

½ teaspoon dried thyme

1 (28-ounce) can diced tomatoes, drained

2 tablespoons tomato paste

1 (15-ounce) can kidney beans, drained and rinsed

Salt and freshly ground black pepper to taste

½ cup freshly grated Parmesan cheese

¼ cup chopped fresh parsley

1 cup grated whole-milk mozzarella cheese

1. Preheat the oven to 400°F, and grease a 10x14-inch baking pan. Bring a large pot of salted water to a boil. Boil pasta according to package directions until al dente. Drain, and place in prepared pan.

2. While pasta cooks, heat a large skillet over medium-high heat. Add sausage and beef, breaking it up with a fork, and brown well. Remove meats from the skillet with a slotted spoon, discard grease, and set aside.

3. Heat oil in the skillet, and add onion and garlic. Cook, stirring frequently, for 3 minutes, or until onion is translucent. Add oregano and thyme, and cook 1 minute, stirring constantly. Add tomatoes, tomato paste, and kidney beans, and simmer 5 minutes. Season to taste with salt and pepper. Stir in Parmesan and parsley, and stir mixture into pasta.
4. Cover the pan with aluminum foil, and bake for 15 minutes. Uncover pan, sprinkle with mozzarella cheese, and bake for an additional 15 minutes, or until bubbly and cheese is melted. Serve immediately.

Note: The dish can be cooked up to 2 days in advance and refrigerated, tightly covered. Reheat, covered with foil, in a 350°F oven for 25–30 minutes, or until hot.

Variations: Like most Italian dishes, this one can be personalized to suit the tastes of the diners around the table:
- Substitute turkey sausage and ground turkey for the beef for a lighter dish.
- Substitute provolone for the mozzarella for a more pronounced cheese flavor.
- While kidney beans are traditional, use whatever beans you have in the pantry.

Garlicky Rosemary Meatballs in Tomato Sauce

Rosemary and garlic are my two favorite seasonings when used together, and they are joined in this recipe to flavor both the meatballs and the heady red wine sauce in which they're cooked. Serve these on some buttered egg noodles.

Yield: 4–6 servings | **Active time:** 20 minutes | **Start to finish:** 45 minutes

> Vegetable oil spray
> 1/4 cup olive oil
> 2 large onions, peeled and chopped
> 5 garlic cloves, peeled and minced
> 1 large egg
> 3 tablespoons whole milk
> 2/3 cup plain breadcrumbs
> 1/4 cup chopped fresh rosemary, divided
> 2 tablespoons chopped fresh parsley
> 1 pound ground chuck
> Salt and freshly ground black pepper to taste
> 1 (15-ounce) can tomato sauce
> 3/4 cup dry red wine

1. Preheat the oven broiler, line a rimmed baking sheet with heavy duty aluminum foil, and spray the foil with vegetable oil spray.

2. Heat oil in a large skillet over medium-high heat. Add onions and garlic and cook, stirring frequently, for 3 minutes, or until onions are translucent. While vegetables cook, combine egg and milk in a mixing bowl, and whisk until smooth. Add breadcrumbs, 2 tablespoons rosemary, and parsley, and mix well.

3. Add 1/2 of onion mixture and beef, season to taste with salt and pepper, and mix well again. Make mixture into 1 1/2-inch meatballs, and arrange meatballs on the prepared pan. Spray tops of meatballs with vegetable oil spray.

4. Broil meatballs 6 inches from the broiler element, turning them with tongs to brown all sides. While meatballs brown, add remaining rosemary, tomato sauce, and wine to the skillet containing remaining onions and garlic. Bring to a boil over medium-high heat, stirring occasionally.

5. Remove meatballs from the baking pan with a slotted spoon, and add meatballs to sauce. Bring to a boil, and simmer meatballs, covered, over low heat, turning occasionally with a slotted spoon, for 15 minutes. Serve immediately.

Note: The beef mixture can be prepared up to 1 day in advance and refrigerated, tightly covered. Also, the dish can be made up to 2 days in advance and refrigerated, tightly covered. Reheat it in a 350°F oven, covered, for 15–20 minutes, or until hot.

Variation: Here's an alteration you can make to this recipe:
- Substitute ground lamb for the ground chuck.

> Onions can be stored in the refrigerator, but they're usually the first food to go if space is at a premium. You can also store them in a cool, dry place on the counter, but don't store them near potatoes. The gas given off by onions will cause potatoes to sprout and rot faster.

One-Step Lasagna

Pre-cooked lasagna noodles are one of the great products to reach supermarkets shelves during the past few years. While this hearty lasagna might look watery as it goes into the oven, it emerges a perfect consistency.

Yield: 6–8 servings | **Active time:** 20 minutes | **Start to finish:** 1¼ hours

1 pound ground chuck
½ pound bulk sweet or hot Italian sausage
2 tablespoons olive oil
1 large onion, peeled and diced
3 garlic cloves, peeled and minced
2 cups Herbed Tomato Sauce (recipe on page 25) or purchased
   marinara sauce
1¾ cups water
3 tablespoons chopped fresh parsley
1 tablespoon Italian seasoning
Salt and freshly ground black pepper to taste
1 (1-pound) box pre-cooked lasagna noodles
1 (15-ounce) container whole-milk ricotta cheese
2 cups grated whole-milk mozzarella cheese
½ cup freshly grated Parmesan cheese

1. Preheat the oven to 350°F, and grease 9x13-inch baking pan.
2. Heat a large skillet over medium-high heat. Add beef and sausage, breaking it up with a fork, and brown well. Remove meats from the skillet with a slotted spoon, discard grease, and set aside. Heat oil in the skillet, and add onion and garlic. Cook, stirring frequently, for 3 minutes, or until onion is translucent.
3. Combine Herbed Tomato Sauce or marinara, water, parsley, and Italian seasoning, and season to taste with salt and pepper. Spread 1½ cups sauce mixture in bottom of the prepared pan. Arrange ⅓ noodles, slightly overlapping if necessary, atop sauce. Spread half of ricotta over noodles. Sprinkle with ½ of mozzarella cheese and top with ½ of meat mixture and 3 tablespoons Parmesan cheese.

Top with 1½ cups sauce. Repeat layering with noodles, ricotta, mozzarella, meats, and Parmesan cheese. Arrange remaining noodles over. Spoon remaining sauce over, covering completely. Sprinkle with remaining Parmesan. Cover pan tightly with aluminum foil. Place on baking sheet.

4. Bake for 50 minutes, or until noodles are tender and dish is bubbly. Remove foil, and bake an additional 10 minutes. Allow to stand for 5 minutes, then serve immediately.

Note: The dish can be prepared up to 2 days in advance and refrigerated, tightly covered. Reheat it in 350°F oven, covered, for 30–40 minutes if chilled.

Be sure to buy the right lasagna noodles for this dish. The precooked noodles are fairly new to the market, and they are what they say: noodles that are partially cooked to rid them of some of the starch, and then dehydrated. Regular lasagna noodles will not cook as well.

Tex-Mex Tamale Pie

This is one of my favorite dishes for a buffet because the cornbread topping crowning the dish is stunning when put on the table. The filling is similar to a chili con carne, and a tossed salad is all you need to complete the meal.

Yield: 4–6 servings | **Active time:** 15 minutes | **Start to finish:** 1 hour

FILLING

- 1 pound ground chuck
- 2 tablespoons olive oil
- 1 large onion, peeled and chopped
- 2 celery ribs, rinsed, trimmed, and sliced
- 1/2 green bell pepper, seeds and ribs removed, and chopped
- 1 jalapeño or serrano chile, seeds and ribs removed, and finely chopped
- 3 garlic cloves, peeled and minced
- 3 tablespoons chili powder
- 1 (14.5-ounce) can diced tomatoes, undrained
- 1 (8-ounce) can tomato sauce
- Salt and freshly ground black pepper to taste
- 1 cup corn kernels, fresh or frozen, thawed

TOPPING

- 2 large eggs, lightly beaten
- 1 cup buttermilk
- 1/4 cup vegetable oil, bacon grease, or melted butter
- 1 1/2 cups yellow cornmeal
- 1/2 cup all-purpose flour
- 2 1/2 teaspoons baking powder
- 1/2 teaspoon salt

1. Preheat the oven to 400°F, and grease a 9x13-inch baking pan.
2. For filling, heat a large skillet over medium-high heat. Add beef, breaking it up with a fork, and brown well. Remove beef from the skillet with a slotted spoon, set aside, and discard grease from the skillet.

3. Heat oil in the skillet, and add onion, celery, bell pepper, chile, and garlic. Cook, stirring frequently, for 3 minutes, or until onion is translucent. Stir in chili powder, and stir 1 minute. Return beef to the skillet, add tomatoes and tomato sauce, and season to taste with salt and pepper. Bring to a boil, and simmer, uncovered, for 10 minutes. Add corn, and simmer 5 minutes. Spread mixture into the prepared pan.
4. While filling simmers, prepare topping. Combine eggs, buttermilk, oil, cornmeal, flour, baking powder, and salt in a mixing bowl, and whisk well. Spoon batter over filling, leaving a ½-inch margin around the edges.
5. Bake for 15 minutes, or until golden. Serve immediately.

Note: The filling can be prepared up to 2 days in advance and refrigerated, tightly covered. Reheat it over low heat until hot before baking.

Variations: Here are some ways to jazz up this dish:
- Instead of corn, use 1 (15-ounce) can kidney beans, drained and rinsed.
- Substitute ground turkey for the ground beef.
- Sprinkle ½ cup grated cheddar or Monterey Jack cheese on top of the cornbread for the last 3 minutes of baking.

> Chili powder is actually a spice blend, and can be made as follows: Combine 2 tablespoons ground red chile, 2 tablespoons paprika, 1 tablespoon ground coriander, 1 tablespoon garlic powder, 1 tablespoon onion powder, 2 teaspoons ground cumin, 2 teaspoons ground red pepper or cayenne, 1 teaspoon ground black pepper, and 1 teaspoon dried oregano.

Italian Stuffed Peppers

Green peppers stuffed with a mixture of beef and cheeses baked in a tomato sauce is a hearty and filling entree that is visually attractive when it comes to the table. I usually serve some pasta, to enjoy all the sauce, and a tossed salad.

Yield: 4–6 servings | **Active time:** 15 minutes | **Start to finish:** 1 hour

4–6 green bell peppers
2 tablespoons olive oil
1 large onion, peeled and chopped
2 garlic cloves, peeled and minced
3 tablespoons chopped fresh parsley
2 teaspoons Italian seasoning
Salt and freshly ground black pepper to taste
1/2 cup breadcrumbs
2 tablespoons whole milk
1/2 cup grated whole-milk mozzarella cheese
1 1/2 cups Herbed Tomato Sauce (recipe on page 25) or purchased marinara sauce, divided
1 large egg, lightly beaten
1 pound ground chuck
1/2 cup freshly grated Parmesan cheese

1. Preheat the oven to 375°F, and grease a 9x13-inch baking pan. Cut off top 1/2 inch of peppers, and reserve. Scoop out seeds and ribs with your hands. Discard stems, and chop flesh from pepper tops.

2. Heat oil in a large skillet over medium-high heat. Add onion, garlic, and chopped pepper pieces. Cook, stirring frequently, for 5 minutes, or until onion softens. Transfer mixture to a large bowl, and add parsley, Italian seasoning, salt, pepper, breadcrumbs, milk, mozzarella, 1/4 cup Herbed Tomato Sauce or marinara sauce, and egg. Mix well, add beef, and mix well again.

3. Fill pepper cavities with beef mixture. Stand peppers up in the pre-pared pan, and pour remaining sauce over them. Cover the pan with aluminum foil, and bake for 25 minutes. Remove the pan from the oven, baste peppers with sauce, and sprinkle with Parmesan cheese. Return pan to the oven, and bake an additional 20 minutes. Serve immediately, spooning sauce over tops of peppers.

Note: The dish can be cooked up to 2 days in advance and refriger-ated, tightly covered. Reheat, covered with foil, in a 350°F oven for 25–30 minutes, or until hot.

Variations: There are many ways to personalize this dish:
- Make it with a combination of beef and Italian sausage.
- Substitute chopped cooked pasta for the breadcrumbs in the recipe.
- Substitute ground pork or ground turkey for the beef.

Spaghetti with Bolognese Sauce

What defines a true Bolognese sauce is the inclusion of both milk and white wine with the vegetables and tomatoes to make the meat in the sauce tender. You can use any pasta you choose.

Yield: 4–6 servings | **Active time:** 15 minutes | **Start to finish:** 1¼ hours

¼ cup olive oil, divided
¾ pound ground chuck
¾ pound ground pork
2 medium onions, peeled and diced
3 celery ribs, rinsed, trimmed, and finely chopped
2 carrots, peeled and finely chopped
4 garlic cloves, peeled and minced
1 (28-ounce) can diced tomatoes, undrained
½ cup whole milk
½ cup dry white wine
¼ cup chopped fresh parsley
1 tablespoon dried oregano
2 teaspoons dried thyme
1 bay leaf
Salt and freshly ground black pepper to taste
1 pound spaghetti
½ cup freshly grated Parmesan cheese

1. Heat 2 tablespoons oil in a heavy 2-quart saucepan over medium-high heat. Add beef and pork, breaking up lumps with a fork. Cook meats for 3 minutes, stirring occasionally, or until no longer pink. Remove meats from the pan with a slotted spoon, and set aside. Discard grease from the pan.

2. Heat remaining 2 tablespoons oil in the pan over medium-high heat. Add onions, celery, carrots, and garlic. Cook, stirring frequently, for 3 minutes, or until onions are translucent. Return meats to the pan and add tomatoes, milk, wine, parsley, oregano, thyme, and bay leaf.

3. Bring to a boil, reduce the heat to low, and simmer sauce, uncovered and stirring occasionally, for 1 hour, or until thickened. Remove and discard bay leaf, and season to taste with salt and pepper.
4. While sauce simmers, bring a large pot of salted water to a boil. Add pasta, and cook according to package directions until al dente. Drain pasta, and top with sauce. Serve immediately, passing Parmesan separately.

Note: The sauce can be prepared up to 3 days in advance and refrigerated, tightly covered. Reheat it over low heat, covered. The sauce can also be frozen for up to 3 months.

Variation: Want to make this dish with less saturated fat?
• Substitute ground turkey for the ground beef and pork.

Shepherd's Pie with Cheddar Potato Topping

While racks of lamb chops clearly fall into the category of luxury foods, it's still possible to enjoy the rich flavor of lamb when using it ground. This classic English dish is quintessential comfort food, and it's very easy to make.

Yield: 4–6 servings | **Active time:** 20 minutes | **Start to finish:** 1¼ hours

FILLING

1 pound ground lamb
2 tablespoons olive oil
1 large onion, peeled and diced
2 garlic cloves, peeled and minced
3 tablespoons all-purpose flour
½ cup dry red wine
½ cup Beef Stock (recipe on page 34) or purchased stock
2 tablespoons chopped fresh parsley
1 tablespoon herbes de Provence
1 (10-ounce) package frozen mixed vegetables, thawed
Salt and freshly ground black pepper to taste

TOPPING

1½ pounds redskin potatoes, scrubbed, and cut into 1-inch dice
⅓ cup heavy cream
2 tablespoons unsalted butter
1 cup grated sharp Cheddar cheese
Salt and freshly ground black pepper to taste

1. Preheat the oven to 400°F, and grease a 9x13-inch baking pan.
2. For filling, heat a large skillet over medium-high heat. Add lamb, breaking up lumps with a fork, and brown well. Remove lamb from the skillet with a slotted spoon, set aside, and discard grease from the skillet.
3. Heat oil in the skillet over medium-high heat. Add onion and garlic, and cook, stirring frequently, for 3 minutes, or until onion is translucent. Stir flour into the skillet, and cook over low heat, stirring constantly, for 2 minutes. Increase the heat to medium-high, and whisk

in wine and stock. Bring to a boil over medium heat, and simmer 2 minutes. Return lamb to the skillet, and add parsley and herbes de Provence. Simmer mixture over low heat, uncovered, for 15 minutes, stirring occasionally. Add vegetables for the last 5 minutes of cooking. Season to taste with salt and pepper.

4. While lamb simmers, prepare topping. Place potatoes in a saucepan of salted water, and bring to a boil over high heat. Reduce the heat to medium and boil potatoes, uncovered, for 12–15 minutes, or until soft. Drain potatoes in a colander. Heat cream, butter, and cheese in the saucepan over medium heat until cheese melts, stirring occasionally. Return potatoes to saucepan, and mash well with a potato masher. Season to taste with salt and pepper. Set aside.

5. Scrape lamb mixture into the prepared pan. Spoon potatoes on top of lamb, smoothing them into an even layer. Bake for 15 minutes, or until the lamb is bubbly and the potatoes are lightly browned. Serve immediately.

Note: The lamb mixture can be prepared up to 2 days in advance and refrigerated, tightly covered; reheat it over low heat before baking. Or the dish can be prepared for baking up to 6 hours in advance and kept at room temperature. Add 5–10 minutes to baking time if lamb is not hot.

Variations: Not fond of lamb? Try this:
- Substitute ground chuck for the ground lamb.
- Make the dish lighter by substituting ground turkey for the lamb.

Greek Lamb and Eggplant (Moussaka)

Topped with a custard sauce, this cinnamon-scented lamb and eggplant filling is a favorite in Greek *tavernas;* I think of it as the Mediterranean version of shepherd's pie. I usually serve it with just a salad because the dish is very rich.

Yield: 6–8 servings | **Active time:** 20 minutes | **Start to finish:** 1½ hours

FILLING

- 1 large eggplant (1½ pounds), cap discarded, and cut into ½-inch dice
- 1½ pounds ground lamb
- ¼ cup olive oil
- 1 large onion, peeled and diced
- 3 garlic cloves, peeled and minced
- 1 (15-ounce) can tomato sauce
- ¾ cup dry red wine
- 2 tablespoons chopped fresh parsley
- 1 teaspoon dried oregano
- ½ teaspoon ground cinnamon
- Salt and freshly ground black pepper to taste

TOPPING

- 4 tablespoons (½ stick) unsalted butter
- ¼ cup all-purpose flour
- 2 cups whole milk
- 3 large eggs, lightly beaten
- ¾ cup freshly grated Parmesan cheese, divided
- 3 tablespoons chopped fresh dill (optional)
- Salt and freshly ground black pepper to taste

1. For filling, place eggplant in a mixing bowl, and cover with heavily salted water; use 1 tablespoon table salt per 1 quart water. Soak eggplant for 30 minutes, then drain and squeeze hard to remove water. Wring out remaining water with cloth tea towel, and set aside.

2. Preheat the oven to 375°F, and grease a 9x13-inch baking pan. Heat a large skillet over medium-high heat. Add lamb, breaking it up with a fork, and brown well. Remove lamb from the skillet with a slotted spoon, set aside, and discard grease from the skillet.

3. Heat oil in the skillet, and add onion and garlic. Cook, stirring frequently, for 3 minutes, or until onion is translucent. Add eggplant, and cook for 3 minutes. Return lamb to the skillet, and add tomato sauce, wine, parsley, oregano, and cinnamon. Simmer for 20 minutes, stirring occasionally. Season to taste with salt and pepper.

4. While lamb simmers, prepare topping. Heat butter in a medium saucepan over low heat. Stir in flour and cook, stirring constantly, for 2 minutes. Whisk in milk, and simmer 2 minutes, or until thick. Whisk ½ cup milk mixture into eggs, then whisk egg mixture back into the saucepan. Remove custard from the stove, and stir in ½ cup Parmesan cheese and dill, if using. Season to taste with salt and pepper.

5. Spread meat mixture into the prepared pan. Pour hot custard cheese sauce over meat, and sprinkle with remaining ¼ cup Parmesan. Bake dish for 45 minutes, or until custard is set and top is browned. Cool 10 minutes, then serve immediately.

Note: The lamb mixture can be prepared up to 2 days in advance and refrigerated, tightly covered; reheat it over low heat before baking. Or the dish can be prepared for baking up to 6 hours in advance and kept at room temperature. Add 5–10 minutes to baking time if lamb is not hot.

While it may seem like a small step, whisking some of the hot liquid into the eggs is crucial to the success of this dish, or any dish done with an egg-enriched custard. It's called "tempering" the eggs, and it makes the sauce smooth rather than like scrambled eggs.

Spicy Chinese Pork Ribs

This is one of the fastest dishes to prepare because there's no need to brown the pork; it will absorb a wonderful color from the sauce. It's spicy but very mellow, and while white rice is always appropriate, I sometimes serve it over angel hair pasta and transform it to a lo mein preparation.

Yield: 4–6 servings | **Active time:** 10 minutes | **Start to finish:** 1 hour

1½ pounds boneless country pork ribs, cut into 1-inch segments
6 scallions, white parts and 4 inches of green tops, rinsed, trimmed, and sliced
2 cups water
¼ cup dry sherry
5 tablespoons Chinese fermented black beans, coarsely chopped*
8 garlic cloves, peeled and minced
2 tablespoons soy sauce
2 tablespoons Asian sesame oil *
1 tablespoon firmly packed dark brown sugar
1 tablespoon cornstarch
1 tablespoon cold water
Crushed red pepper flakes to taste

1. Place pork and scallions in a saucepan. Combine water, sherry, black beans, garlic, soy sauce, sesame oil, and brown sugar in a small bowl, and stir well. Pour mixture over ribs.

2. Bring to a boil over medium-high heat, stirring occasionally. Reduce the heat to low, cover the pan, and cook pork for 50–55 minutes, or until very tender. Mix cornstarch and water in a small cup, and stir mixture into stew. Cook for 1–2 minutes, or until slightly thickened. Season to taste with crushed red pepper, and serve immediately.

* Available in the Asian aisle of most supermarkets and in specialty markets.

Note: The dish can be cooked up to 2 days in advance and refrigerated, tightly covered. Reheat it over low heat until simmering.

Variations: This recipe is one of the most versatile in the book, because a number of different types of protein are delicious when cooked this way; what varies is the cooking times:

- Use cubes of beef in place of the pork ribs. Brown the beef under the oven broiler before cooking, and the cooking time will be about 2 hours.
- Use boneless, skinless chicken thighs, and the cooking time will be the same as for pork.

Fermented black beans are small black soybeans with a pungent flavor that have been preserved in salt before being packed. They should be chopped and soaked in some sort of liquid such as water or sherry to soften them and release their flavor prior to cooking. Because they are salted as a preservative, they last for up to 2 years if refrigerated once opened.

Braised Pork Chops with Red Cabbage

Cabbage is one of the oldest vegetables in recorded history, although its stature has ranged from lowly to esteemed depending on the culture. In this case pork chops become meltingly tender when cooked with bright red cabbage, which has a slightly sweet and sour flavor.

Yield: 4–6 servings | **Active time:** 15 minutes | **Start to finish:** 1 hour

- 4–6 boneless pork loin chops, trimmed of fat, rinsed, and patted dry with paper towels
- Salt and freshly ground black pepper to taste
- 2 tablespoons vegetable oil
- 1 onion, peeled and chopped
- 2 Golden Delicious apples, cored, peeled, and cut into 1/2-inch dice
- 1 cup Chicken Stock (recipe on page 33) or purchased stock
- 1/2 cup dry red wine
- 2 tablespoons cider vinegar
- 3 tablespoons firmly packed dark brown sugar
- 1 (3-inch) cinnamon stick
- 1 bay leaf
- 1 (2-pound) head red cabbage, cored and shredded
- 1/3 cup red currant jelly

1. Sprinkle chops with salt and pepper. Heat oil in a deep-sided skillet over medium-high heat. Add pork, and cook, turning pieces with tongs, until brown on both sides. Remove pork from the pan with tongs, and set aside.

2. Add onion and apples to the skillet, and cook, stirring frequently, for 3 minutes, or until onion is translucent. Add stock, wine, vinegar, sugar, cinnamon stick, and bay leaf. Bring to a boil, and stir in the cabbage. Bring to a boil, and simmer, uncovered, for 5 minutes.

3. Bury chops in cabbage, cover the pan, and cook over low heat for 30–45 minutes, or until the cabbage is tender. Remove chops from the pan, remove and discard cinnamon stick and bay leaf, and stir jelly into cabbage. Cook, uncovered, over medium heat for 10 minutes, or until the liquid reduces and becomes syrupy. Return chops to pan, and heat through.

Note: The dish can be cooked up to 2 days in advance and refrigerated, tightly covered. Reheat it over low heat until simmering.

Old-Fashioned Pork and Beans

Baked beans are so interwoven into Boston's history that it's still known as "Beantown." I sometimes double this recipe except for the amount of pork, and I freeze the leftover beans to use in the future as a side dish.

Yield: 4-6 servings | **Active time:** 15 minutes | **Start to finish:** 4 hours

1 pound dried small navy beans, rinsed
2 tablespoons vegetable oil
1 pound boneless country ribs, cut into 1-inch cubes, rinsed, and
    patted dry with paper towels
Salt and freshly ground black pepper to taste
1 large onion, peeled and diced
6 cups water
1 cup ketchup
$\frac{1}{3}$ cup molasses
$\frac{1}{4}$ cup cider vinegar
$\frac{1}{4}$ cup firmly packed dark brown sugar
1 tablespoon dry mustard powder

1. Soak beans in cold water to cover for a minimum of 6 hours, or preferably overnight. Or, place beans in a saucepan covered with water, and bring to a boil over high heat. Boil for 1 minute, turn off the heat, and cover the pan. Allow beans to soak for 1 hour, then drain. With either method, continue with the dish as soon as beans have soaked, or refrigerate beans.

2. Preheat the oven to 350°F. Heat oil in a Dutch oven over medium-high heat. Sprinkle pork with salt and pepper. Add pork, and cook, turning pieces with tongs, until brown on all sides. Remove pork from the pan with a slotted spoon, and set aside.

3. Add onion to the pan, and cook, stirring frequently, for 3 minutes, or until onion is translucent. Return pork to the pan and add beans, water, ketchup, molasses, vinegar, brown sugar, and mustard powder. Bring to a boil, cover the pan, and bake for 1 hour.

4. Uncover the pan, stir, and return the pan to the oven for $2\frac{1}{2}$-3 hours, or until beans are very tender and dish is thick. Serve immediately.

Note: The dish can be cooked up to 2 days in advance and refrigerated, tightly covered. Reheat, covered with foil, in a 350°F oven for 25-30 minutes, or until hot.

New Mexican Pork and Hominy Stew (Pozole)

Corn is the quintessentially American food, and was raised by Native American tribes from the Atlantic to the Pacific. This dish is relatively quick to make because it uses canned hominy, so soaking the kernels is not necessary.

Yield: 4–6 servings | **Active time:** 15 minutes | **Start to finish:** 2½ hours

1½ pounds boneless pork loin, cut into 1-inch cubes, rinsed, and patted dry with paper towels
Salt and freshly ground black pepper to taste
2 tablespoons olive oil
1 large onion, peeled and diced
2 garlic cloves, peeled and minced
1 small jalapeño or serrano chile, seeds and ribs removed, and finely chopped
2 tablespoons chili powder
2 teaspoons ground cumin
1½ cups Chicken Stock (recipe on page 33) or purchased stock
1 (14.5-ounce) can diced tomatoes, undrained
2 (15-ounce) cans yellow hominy, drained and rinsed well
1 cup fresh corn kernels or frozen corn kernels, thawed
Sour cream
Lime wedges

1. Preheat the oven to 350°F. Sprinkle pork with salt and pepper. Heat oil in a Dutch oven over medium-high heat. Add pork, and cook, turning pieces with tongs, until brown on all sides. Remove pork from the pan with tongs, and set aside.

2. Add onion, garlic, and chile to the pan, and cook, stirring frequently, for 3 minutes, or until onion is translucent. Stir in chili powder and cumin, and cook, stirring constantly, for 1 minute. Return meat to pan, and stir in stock and tomatoes. Bring to a boil over medium-high heat. Cover the pan, and bake for 1 hour. Add hominy and corn, and bake for 1 hour, or until pork is very tender. Serve immediately, passing bowls of sour cream and lime wedges.

Note: The dish can be cooked up to 2 days in advance and refrigerated, tightly covered. Reheat, covered, in a 350°F oven for 25–30 minutes, or until hot.

Pork is much more delicate in flavor and lighter in color than beef or lamb, so the stock that should be used for pork dishes is chicken rather than beef stock. Pork is rarely, if ever, made into a stock of its own, although smoked ham bones can be used to flavor stocks and soups.

Vietnamese Pork Loin

This is a totally succulent pork roast marinated in a richly flavored mix of Asian seasonings. Serve it with some rice and stir-fried vegetables.

Yield: 6–8 servings | **Active time:** 15 minutes | **Start to finish:** 6 hours, including 4 hours for marinating

> 1 (3-pound) boneless center cut pork loin
> 3 stalks lemongrass
> 4 scallions, white parts only, rinsed, trimmed, and sliced
> 4 garlic cloves, peeled
> 1 jalapeño or serrano chile, seeds and ribs removed
> ½ cup vegetable oil, divided
> ¼ cup soy sauce
> ¼ cup fish sauce (*nam pla*)*
> ¼ cup sherry
> 3 tablespoons firmly packed light brown sugar
> Freshly ground black pepper to taste

1. Rinse pork and pat dry with paper towels. Discard outer leaves from lemongrass, trim root end, and slice bottom 4 inches of bulb.
2. Combine lemongrass, scallions, garlic, chile, ¼ cup oil, soy sauce, fish sauce, sherry, sugar, and pepper in a blender or food processor fitted with a steel blade. Puree until smooth. Pour mixture into a heavy resealable plastic bag, and add pork. Marinate pork, refrigerated, for 4–12 hours, turning the bag occasionally.
3. Preheat the oven to 350°F. Heat remaining oil in a roasting pan over medium-high heat. Remove pork from marinade, and discard marinade. Pat roast dry with paper towels. Sear roast in oil, turning with tongs, until brown on all sides.

* Available in the Asian aisle of most supermarkets and in specialty markets.

4. Roast pork, uncovered, for 45–60 minutes, or until the temperature registers 150°F on an instant-read thermometer. Remove pork from the oven and place it on a platter, loosely covered with aluminum foil. Allow pork to rest for 15 minutes to allow juices to be reabsorbed into meat. Then slice thinly against the grain, and serve immediately.

Note: The roast can be baked up to 6 hours in advance and kept at room temperature.

Variation: Like this marinade? Then try this, too:
- Marinate chicken pieces for 4–10 hours, and bake for 40–45 minutes, or until cooked through and no longer pink.

Lemongrass, which is botanically an herb, although it resembles a dried out scallion, adds a spicy citrus flavor to foods. While it is now easy to find in most supermarkets, if you can't find it you can substitute 1 tablespoon lemon juice and ¼ teaspoon ground ginger for each stalk of lemongrass.

Basic Italian-American Meatballs

After years of experimentation, I've settled on this recipe as my favorite meatball. It has a complex flavor profile from the mixture of herbs and spices it contains, as well as cheeses that add moisture, too.

Yield: 4–6 servings | **Active time:** 20 minutes | **Start to finish:** 50 minutes

Vegetable oil spray
2 tablespoons olive oil
1 small onion, peeled and finely chopped
3 garlic cloves, peeled and minced
¼ teaspoon crushed red pepper flakes
1 large egg
3 tablespoons whole milk
⅔ cup seasoned Italian breadcrumbs
⅓ cup freshly grated Parmesan cheese
⅓ cup grated whole-milk mozzarella cheese
3 tablespoons chopped fresh parsley
1 teaspoon Italian seasoning
½ teaspoon dried thyme
½ pound ground pork
½ pound ground chuck
Salt and freshly ground black pepper to taste
2 cups Herbed Tomato Sauce (recipe on page 25) or purchased
   marinara sauce

1. Preheat the oven broiler, line a rimmed baking sheet with heavy duty aluminum foil, and spray the foil with vegetable oil spray.
2. Heat oil in a large skillet over medium-high heat. Add onion, garlic, and red pepper flakes, and cook, stirring frequently, for 3 minutes, or until onion is translucent.
3. Combine egg and milk in a mixing bowl, and whisk until smooth. Add breadcrumbs, Parmesan cheese, mozzarella cheese, parsley, Italian seasoning, and thyme, and mix well.
4. Add onion mixture, pork, and beef, season to taste with salt and pepper, and mix well again. Make mixture into 1½-inch meatballs, and arrange meatballs on the prepared pan. Spray tops of meatballs with vegetable oil spray.

5. Broil meatballs 6 inches from the broiler element, turning them with tongs to brown all sides. While meatballs brown, heat Herbed Tomato Sauce or marinara sauce in the skillet in which vegetables cooked.

6. Remove meatballs from the baking pan with a slotted spoon, and add meatballs to sauce. Bring to a boil, reduce heat to low, and simmer meatballs, covered, turning occasionally with a slotted spoon, for 15 minutes. Season to taste with salt and pepper, and serve immediately.

Note: The meatball mixture can be prepared up to 1 day in advance and refrigerated, tightly covered. Also, the dish can be cooked up to 2 days in advance and refrigerated, tightly covered. Reheat in a 350°F oven, covered, for 15–20 minutes, or until hot.

Variations: A supply of cooked meatballs in the freezer is the basis for a treasure trove of dishes. Here are some ways to use them:

- For the traditional spaghetti and meatballs, just cook ½ to 1 pound of your favorite pasta, and pass some freshly grated Parmesan cheese on the side.
- Cut the cooked meatballs into small pieces and use them to top a pizza.
- For a meatball sandwich, make an indentation in the center of a roll or section of bread to accommodate the size of the meatballs. Then top the meatballs with grated or sliced mozzarella cheese and bake the sandwich in a 375°F oven for 10 to 12 minutes or until meatballs are hot and cheese melts.

Spaghetti with Egg and Bacon (*Pasta Carbonara*)

It takes longer for the water to come to a boil to cook the pasta than it does to create this classic Italian dish that's spicy with black pepper, and rich from eggs and cheese. A tossed salad is all you need to complete the meal.

Yield: 4–6 servings | **Active time:** 15 minutes | **Start to finish:** 25 minutes

> ³/₄ pound spaghetti
> ³/₄ pound bacon, sliced into ¹/₂-inch lengths
> 6 garlic cloves, peeled and minced
> Freshly ground black pepper to taste (at least 1¹/₂ teaspoons)
> 6 large eggs, beaten
> 1 ¹/₂ cups freshly grated Parmesan cheese
> Salt to taste

1. Bring a large pot of salted water to a boil. Add pasta, and cook according to package directions until al dente. Drain, and set aside.

2. While water heats, place bacon in a heavy 12-inch skillet over medium-high heat. Cook, stirring occasionally, for 5–7 minutes, or until crisp. Remove bacon from the skillet with a slotted spoon, and set aside. Discard all but 2 tablespoons bacon grease from the pan. Add garlic and black pepper, and cook for 30 seconds. Return bacon to the pan, and turn off heat.

3. Add drained pasta to the skillet, and cook over medium heat for 1 minute. Remove the pan from the stove, and stir in eggs. Allow eggs to thicken but do not put the pan back on the stove or they will scramble. Add cheese, and season to taste with salt and additional pepper. Serve immediately.

The last place you want your food dollars to go is to an expensive visit from the plumber, and bacon grease is notorious for clogging kitchen plumbing, even if it's put down the sink with hot water running. Rinse out empty half-pint cream containers and keep them under the sink. Pour unwanted bacon fat into a bowl, and after it cools dispose of it in the container.

Italian Ham and Vegetables

When baked ham is cooked further it becomes meltingly tender and succulent; the vegetables and Italian tomato sauce render it that way. Serve this with pasta to enjoy the sauce, and a tossed salad.

Yield: 4–6 servings | **Active time:** 15 minutes | **Start to finish:** 45 minutes

   2 tablespoons olive oil
   2 large onions, peeled and thinly sliced
   3 garlic cloves, peeled and minced
   1 green bell pepper, seeds and ribs removed, and thinly sliced
   1 (14.5-ounce) can crushed tomatoes in tomato puree
   ¾ cup Chicken Stock (recipe on page 33) or purchased stock
   ¼ cup dry red wine
   2 tablespoons chopped fresh parsley
   1 tablespoon Italian seasoning
   1 bay leaf
   1 pound baked ham, cut into thick slices, or ham steaks
   Salt and freshly ground black pepper to taste

1. Heat oil in a medium skillet over medium-high heat. Add onions, garlic, and green bell pepper, and cook, stirring frequently, for 3 minutes, or until onions are translucent.
2. Add tomatoes, stock, wine, parsley, Italian seasoning, and bay leaf, and bring to a boil over medium-high heat, stirring occasionally. Reduce the heat to low and simmer mixture, covered, for 15 minutes. Add ham, and simmer an additional 15 minutes, or until vegetables are soft. Remove and discard bay leaf, season to taste with salt and pepper, and serve immediately.

Note: The dish can be cooked up to 2 days in advance and refrigerated, tightly covered. Reheat it over low heat until simmering.

Cajun Stewed Red Beans and Ham

Red beans and rice are so much a part of Louisiana's culinary heritage that famed jazz musician Louis Armstrong used to sign his letters, "Red beans and ricely yours." The red beans in this recipe should be served on rice, which adds to their protein content.

Yield: 4–6 servings | **Active time:** 15 minutes | **Start to finish:** 2 hours, including 1 hour to soak the beans

> 1 pound dried red kidney beans, rinsed
> 2 tablespoons bacon grease or vegetable oil
> 2 medium onions, peeled and finely chopped
> 2 celery ribs, rinsed, trimmed, and finely chopped
> 1 green bell pepper, seeds and ribs removed, and finely chopped
> 2 garlic cloves, peeled and minced
> 1 tablespoon paprika
> 2 bay leaves
> 2 teaspoons dried thyme
> 6 cups water
> 1 pound cooked ham, trimmed of fat and cut into $\frac{1}{2}$-inch dice
> Salt and freshly ground black pepper to taste
> Hot red pepper sauce to taste

1. Soak beans in cold water to cover for a minimum of 6 hours, or preferably overnight. Or, place beans in a saucepan covered with water, and bring to a boil over high heat. Boil for 1 minute, turn off the heat, and cover the pan. Allow beans to soak for 1 hour, then drain. With either method, continue with the dish as soon as beans have soaked, or refrigerate beans.

2. Heat bacon grease or oil in a 3-quart saucepan over medium-high heat. Add onions, celery, green pepper, and garlic, and cook, stirring frequently, for 3 minutes, or until onions are translucent. Add paprika, bay leaves, and thyme, and cook over low heat for 1 minute, stirring constantly.

3. Return beans to the pan, add water, and bring to a boil, stirring occasionally. Reduce the heat to low, cover the pan, and simmer beans for 45 minutes. Add ham, and simmer an additional 15–30 minutes, or until beans are very soft. Remove and discard bay leaves, and season to taste with salt, pepper, and hot red pepper sauce. Serve immediately.

Note: The dish can be made up to 2 days in advance and refrigerated, tightly covered. Reheat it over low heat or in a 350°F oven for 30 minutes, or until hot.

Variation: Want to serve this vegetarian?
- Omit the ham and use vegetable oil.

If you're not too worried about cholesterol, save the bacon grease that emerges when you cook bacon, and use it in cooking. It adds a smoky nuance to dishes, and it's free—you've already purchased the bacon!

Potato, Onion, and Bacon Frittata

In classic French cooking the joining of bacon, potatoes, and sautéed onion dubs a dish Lyonnaise, after the city of Lyons. It's a flavorful combination, and it's equally at home in a frittata for brunch or supper as garnishing a piece of fish or chicken.

Yield: 4–6 servings | **Active time:** 20 minutes | **Start to finish:** 40 minutes

> ½ pound bacon, cut into 1-inch lengths
> 2 large redskin potatoes, scrubbed and cut into 1/4-inch dice
> 1 large onion, peeled and diced
> 8 large eggs
> ¼ cup half-and-half
> 2 tablespoons chopped fresh parsley
> ½ teaspoon dried thyme
> Salt and freshly ground black pepper to taste
> 2 tablespoons unsalted butter

1. Place bacon in a skillet over medium-high heat. Cook for 5–7 minutes, or until bacon is crisp. Remove bacon from the pan with a slotted spoon, drain on paper towels, and set aside.
2. Discard all but 3 tablespoons bacon fat from the skillet. Add potatoes, and cook for 5 minutes, or until potatoes are tender, scraping them occasionally with a heavy spatula. Add onion to the skillet, and cook for 5 minutes, stirring occasionally, or until onion is soft. Allow mixture to cool for 10 minutes.
3. Preheat the oven to 425°F. Whisk eggs and half-and-half well, stir in parsley and thyme, and season to taste with salt and pepper. Stir bacon and cooled vegetable mixture into eggs. Heat butter in a large, oven-proof skillet over medium heat. Add egg mixture and cook for 4 minutes, or until the bottom of cake is lightly brown. Transfer the skillet to the oven, and bake for 10–15 minutes, or until top is browned.

4. Run a spatula around the sides of the skillet and under the bottom of the cake to release it. Slide cake gently onto a serving platter, and cut it into wedges. Serve immediately or at room temperature.

Note: The vegetable mixture can be cooked up to 1 day in advance and refrigerated, tightly covered. Reheat the vegetables to room temperature in a microwave-safe dish, or over low heat, before completing the dish.

Variations: Here are some ways to vary this basic dish:
- Substitute ham or sausage for the bacon.
- Add ½ cup diced red bell pepper to the dish, and cook it along with the onion and garlic.

Having trouble separating individual slices of bacon without tearing them? If so, try this: Peel off the total number of slices you need and place the block into the hot pan. Within a few minutes the slices will naturally separate from the heat, and then you can pull them apart.

Spanish Frittata

This frittata is a first cousin to a Spanish tortilla, which is an omelet served at tapas bars and not a bread like a Latin American tortilla. Don't throw out any leftovers from this dish; refrigerate it, and cut it into small squares to serve as a snack.

Yield: 4–6 servings | **Active time:** 20 minutes | **Start to finish:** 45 minutes

> 2 tablespoons olive oil
> 1 large redskin potato, scrubbed and cut into 1/2-inch dice
> 1 green bell pepper, seeds and ribs removed, and chopped
> 1 large sweet onion, such as Bermuda or Vidalia, peeled and diced
> 1 cup chopped baked ham
> 2 garlic cloves, peeled and minced
> Salt and freshly ground black pepper to taste
> 8 large eggs
> 1/4 cup freshly grated Parmesan cheese
> 1/4 cup grated whole milk mozzarella cheese
> 1 teaspoon Italian seasoning
> 2 tablespoons unsalted butter

1. Heat olive oil in a large skillet over medium-high heat. Add potatoes, and cook, stirring occasionally, for 5 minutes, or until potatoes are browned. Add bell pepper, onion, ham, and garlic to the skillet. Cook, stirring constantly, for 3 minutes, or until onion is translucent. Reduce the heat to low, cover the pan, and cook vegetable mixture for 15 minutes, or until the vegetables are tender. Season to taste with salt and pepper, and allow mixture to cool for 10 minutes.

2. Preheat the oven to 425°F. Whisk eggs well, stir in Parmesan and mozzarella cheeses, and Italian seasoning. Stir cooled vegetable mixture into eggs. Heat butter in a large, oven-proof skillet over medium heat. Add egg mixture and cook for 4 minutes, or until the bottom of cake is lightly brown. Transfer the skillet to the oven, and bake for 10–15 minutes, or until top is browned.

3. Run a spatula around the sides of the skillet and under the bottom of the cake to release it. Slide cake gently onto a serving platter, and cut it into wedges. Serve immediately or at room temperature.

Note: The vegetable mixture can be cooked up to 1 day in advance and refrigerated, tightly covered. Reheat the vegetables to room temperature in a microwave-safe dish, or over low heat, before completing the dish.

While the cost of eggs has risen with every other food, they still represent an excellent value because they are considered nutrient dense; they provide excellent protein and a wide range of vitamins and minerals in proportion to their 75 to 80 calories per egg. Egg protein is a complete protein and contains all the essential amino acids in a pattern that matches very closely the pattern the body needs.

Ham and Cheese Frittata

You'll find many recipes in this book that take advantage of leftover ham. Baked ham is usually an inexpensive option, and baking a larger ham gives you fodder for more food, like this easy and delicious frittata.

Yield: 4–6 servings | **Active time:** 15 minutes | **Start to finish:** 30 minutes

>   3 tablespoons unsalted butter
>   2 scallions, white parts and 2 inches of green tops, rinsed, trimmed, and chopped
>   1 large green bell pepper, seeds and ribs removed, and chopped
>   1 cup chopped baked ham
>   ¼ cup chopped fresh chives
>   8 large eggs
>   1 cup grated sharp cheddar cheese
>   Salt and freshly ground black pepper to taste

1. Preheat the oven to 425°F. Heat butter in an oven-proof skillet over medium-high heat. Add scallions, green pepper, ham, and chives. Cook, stirring frequently, for 5 minutes, or until vegetables soften.
2. Whisk eggs well, stir in cheese, and season to taste with salt and pepper. Add egg mixture to the skillet, and cook over medium heat for 4 minutes, or until bottom of cake is lightly brown. Transfer the skillet to the oven, and bake for 10–15 minutes, or until top is browned.
3. Run a spatula around the sides of the skillet and under the bottom of the cake to release it. Slide cake gently onto a serving platter, and cut it into wedges. Serve immediately, or at room temperature.

Note: The vegetable mixture can be cooked up to 1 day in advance and refrigerated, tightly covered. Reheat the vegetables to room temperature in a microwave-safe dish, or over low heat, before completing the dish.

Herbed Sausage and Tomato Quiche

Quiche got a bad reputation after the publication in 1982 of Bruce Feirstein's satirical look at masculinity, *Real Men Don't Eat Quiche.* I can assure you that the men around my table gobble up this hearty custard pie loaded with sausage and herbs.

Yield: 4–6 servings | **Active time:** 15 minutes | **Start to finish:** 40 minutes

> 1 (9-inch single) Basic Pie Crust (recipe on page 227) or purchased pie shell, thawed if frozen
> ³/₄ pound bulk pork sausage
> 1 small onion, peeled and chopped
> 3 garlic cloves, peeled and minced
> 1 (14.5-ounce) can petite cut canned tomatoes, drained
> 3 large eggs
> 1 cup (½ pint) heavy cream
> Salt and freshly ground black pepper to taste

1. Preheat the oven to 400°F. Prick pie shell all over with the tines of a fork and bake for 8–10 minutes, or until pastry is set and just starting to brown. Remove crust from the oven, and set aside.
2. While crust bakes, place a large skillet over medium-high heat, and crumble sausage into it, breaking up any lumps with a fork. Cook sausage, stirring occasionally, for 5 minutes, or until sausage is brown and no pink remains. Add onion and garlic and cook, stirring frequently, for 3 minutes, or until onion is translucent. Add tomatoes and cook, stirring occasionally, for 5–7 minutes, or until tomato juice has evaporated. Cool mixture for 5 minutes.
3. Reduce the oven temperature to 375°F. Whisk eggs with cream, and season to taste with salt and pepper. Stir in sausage mixture, fill pie shell, and bake quiche for 25 – 30 minutes, or until it is browned and eggs are set. Serve immediately.

Note: The filling can be prepared 1 day in advance and refrigerated, tightly covered. Add 5–7 minutes to the baking time if filling is chilled.

Variation: Here's another way to use the flavors in this recipe:
- Chopped ham or poultry sausage can be substituted for the pork sausage. The ham requires no pre-cooking.

Mac' and Cheese with Ham

While Italians have all sorts of pasta dishes made with cheeses, mac' and cheese is our home-grown American favorite. Delicious in and of itself, it's also a great way to use up leftover ham.

Yield: 6–8 servings | **Active time:** 15 minutes | **Start to finish:** 50 minutes

1 pound elbow macaroni
4 tablespoons (½ stick) unsalted butter
¼ cup all-purpose flour
1 tablespoon paprika
1 teaspoon dry mustard powder
½ cup Chicken Stock (recipe on page 33) or purchased stock
2½ cups whole milk
1 pound grated sharp cheddar cheese, divided
Salt and freshly ground black pepper to taste
1 pound cooked ham, trimmed of fat and cut into ½-inch cubes

1. Preheat the oven to 375°F, and grease a 9x13-inch baking pan. Bring a large pot of salted water to a boil. Add macaroni, and cook for 2 minutes less than package directions. Drain, and place macaroni in the prepared pan.

2. While macaroni cooks, melt butter in a saucepan over low heat. Stir in flour, paprika, and mustard, and stir constantly for 2 minutes. Whisk in chicken stock, and bring to a boil over medium-high heat, whisking constantly. Whisk in milk, and bring to a boil again, stirring frequently. Reduce the heat to low and simmer for 2 minutes. Stir in all but ½ cup grated cheese, stirring until cheese melts, and season to taste with salt and pepper.

3. Stir ham and sauce into macaroni, and sprinkle with remaining ½ cup cheese. Bake for 25–30 minutes, or until bubbly. Allow to sit for 5 minutes, then serve immediately.

Note: The dish can be prepared up to baking 2 days in advance and refrigerated, tightly covered. Reheat it, covered with foil, for 15 minutes before removing foil and baking for 25 minutes.

Variations: Try these modifications:
- Substitute cooked chicken or turkey for the ham.
- Make the dish vegetarian by adding 2 cups sautéed mushrooms instead of ham.

Chapter 7:
Vegetarian with Verve

Dishes made with healthful beans, grains, pasta, and vegetables are the focus of the recipes in this chapter. And the good news is that all of them are basically inexpensive, even in the worst of economic times.

Perhaps you now count yourself among the growing group of "occasional vegetarians" who eschew animal protein one or two nights a week. Then look at this chapter carefully. But many of these recipes can also be served as side dishes to elevate a simple baked or broiled entree to a new level of elegance. If served as a side dish rather than a main course, the yield would be double what is listed.

WHERE HAVE YOU BEAN?

Beans are justly praised for their nutritional value as well as their availability and economy, and dried beans play a role in almost all the world's cuisines. Beans are a high source of fiber and protein, and they are low in fat and contain no cholesterol. They are also a good source of B vitamins, especially B6.

Before using beans, rinse them in a colander or sieve under cold running water, and pick through them to discard any broken beans or pebbles that might have found their way into the bag. Then there's a secondary step once the beans have been covered with water; discard any that float to the top.

Dried beans should be cooked until they are no longer crunchy, but still have texture. If beans are going to be cooked and then cooked further in a dish, such as in a chili, then stop the initial cooking when they are still slightly crunchy. The other caveat of bean cookery is to make sure beans are cooked to the proper consistency before adding any acidic ingredient, such as tomatoes or lemon, because acid prevents the beans from becoming tender.

PASTA POWER

There are also many recipes in this chapter for vegetarian pasta dishes. Good-quality dried pasta is made with a high percentage of semolina, the inner part of the grain of hard durum wheat. The gluten gives the pasta resilience, and allows it to cook while remaining somewhat firm, thus reaching the elusive state of al dente. The higher the semolina content of pasta, the more protein it will contain.

As a general rule, pasta imported from Italy is superior to American products due to its higher semolina percentage. Try to purchase pasta that you can see behind cellophane in a box. The pasta should be smooth and shiny, and not crumbly. Store pastas in sealed plastic bags once the boxes are opened. Pasta will stay fresh for at least 6 months. But even many months later, it's safe to use as long as it hasn't developed mold. Stale pasta takes a bit longer to cook, however.

COMPLETING PROTEINS

The reason why there are so many dishes that pair beans with rice or pasta is more than flavor. What generations before us knew instinctively, and we now know scientifically, is that the protein in legumes such as beans is "incomplete." This means that in order to deliver its best nutritional content, beans need to be paired with carbohydrate-rich grains such as rice. When the beans and grains are eaten together, they supply a quality of protein that's as good as that from eggs or beef.

Italian Bread and Tomato Stew (*Pappa al Pomodoro*)

Aromatic from fresh basil, creamy with cheeses, and hearty with heart-healthy tomatoes, this thick bread stew is the epitome of Italian comfort food. Serve it with a green salad, and your meal is complete.

Yield: 6–8 servings | **Active time:** 15 minutes | **Start to finish:** 40 minutes

- $3/4$ pound loaf Italian or French bread
- 3 cups whole milk
- $1/4$ cup olive oil
- 1 large onion, peeled and diced
- 2 garlic cloves, peeled and chopped
- 2 (28-ounce) cans diced tomatoes, drained
- $1/2$ cup firmly packed chopped fresh basil
- $1/2$ cup grated whole-milk mozzarella cheese
- $1/2$ cup freshly grated Parmesan cheese
- Salt and freshly ground black pepper to taste

1. Break or cut bread into 1-inch cubes. Place cubes in a mixing bowl, and add milk, stirring to press all cubes into liquid.
2. Heat olive oil in a 3-quart saucepan over medium-high heat. Add onion and garlic, and cook, stirring frequently, for 3 minutes, or until onion is translucent. Add tomatoes and cook for 10 minutes, stirring occasionally.
3. Add bread mixture and basil to the saucepan, and bring to a boil over medium-high heat, stirring frequently. Reduce the heat to low, and simmer mixture, uncovered, for 15 minutes. Stir in mozzarella and Parmesan, and simmer for 3 minutes, stirring frequently. Season to taste with salt and pepper, and serve immediately.

Note: The dish can be made up to 2 days in advance and refrigerated, tightly covered. Reheat it over low heat, covered, until hot, stirring occasionally.

Greek Pasta with Oven-Roasted Tomato Sauce

Oven-roasting tomatoes caramelizes their natural sugars, and intensifies their flavor. Some of the liquid evaporates, and the tomatoes are rendered tender, too. This is a light pasta dish, perfect for summer when tomatoes are in season, and reasonably priced.

Yield: 4–6 servings | **Active time:** 15 minutes | **Start to finish:** 1 hour

> 3 pounds ripe plum tomatoes, rinsed, cored, seeded, and diced
> ⅓ cup olive oil
> 5 garlic cloves, peeled and minced
> 1 tablespoon balsamic vinegar
> 1 tablespoon dried oregano
> 2 teaspoons dried basil
> ½ teaspoon crushed red pepper flakes
> Salt and freshly ground black pepper to taste
> ¾ pound linguine
> ½ cup chopped pitted Kalamata olives, or other brine-cured olives
> ¼ pound feta cheese, crumbled

1. Preheat the oven to 375°F, and grease a 9x13-inch baking pan.
2. Combine tomatoes, oil, garlic, vinegar, oregano, basil, and crushed red pepper in the prepared pan, and season to taste with salt and pepper. Roast tomatoes for 45 minutes, or until tomatoes are tender and juicy, stirring occasionally.
3. While tomatoes bake, bring a large pot of salted water to a boil over high heat. Cook linguine according to package directions until al dente. Return pasta to pot, and add tomato mixture, olives, and feta. Stir over medium heat until heated through and feta is melted and creamy, about 3 minutes. Serve immediately.

Note: The tomatoes can be baked up to 2 days in advance and refrigerated, tightly covered. Reheat them over low heat before tossing with pasta.

Spaghetti with Raisins and Endive

This fast and easy pasta dish contrasts sweet raisins with slightly bitter curly endive in a very light white wine sauce. Children adore it, too.

Yield: 6–8 servings | **Active time:** 10 minutes | **Start to finish:** 25 minutes

    1 pound spaghetti
    ½ cup raisins
    1 (1-pound) head curly endive
    ⅓ cup olive oil
    4 garlic cloves, peeled and minced
    ¼ cup dry white wine
    ¼ cup water
    Salt and freshly ground black pepper to taste
    ¾ cup freshly grated Parmesan cheese

1. Bring a large pot of salted water to a boil. Add pasta, and cook according to package directions until al dente. Drain, reserving ½ cup of cooking liquid, and set aside. Soak raisins in very hot tap water for 15 minutes, then drain and set aside. Rinse curly endive well, discard the core, and cut it into thin shreds. Set aside.

2. While water heats, heat olive oil in a heavy, large skillet over medium heat. Add garlic to the skillet and cook, stirring constantly, for 1 minute. Add raisins, endive, wine, and water to the skillet. Stir well, cover the skillet, and cook, stirring occasionally, for 10 minutes, or until endive is soft. Season to taste with salt and pepper.

3. Add drained pasta to the skillet, and add some reserved cooking water if mixture seems dry. Cook for 2 minutes. Serve immediately, passing Parmesan cheese separately.

Note: The pasta can be cooked and the sauce mixture can be prepared up to 4 hours in advance and kept at room temperature. Add a few minutes to the final cooking time if the pasta is cool.

Variation: For a non-vegetarian dish, try this addition:
- Brown ½ pound bulk Italian sausage before adding the garlic to the skillet, and cook the sausage with the endive.

Pasta with Garlic and Oil (*Pasta Aglio e Olio*)

Getting a delicious dinner on the table doesn't get any easier than this recipe! As long as you cook with garlic, you've probably got everything you need right in the kitchen, so as soon as the pasta is cooked you're ready to eat.

Yield: 6–8 servings | **Active time:** 10 minutes | **Start to finish:** 25 minutes

1 pound spaghetti or linguine
2/3 cup olive oil
10 garlic cloves, peeled and minced
1–1 1/2 teaspoons crushed red pepper flakes
Salt to taste
3/4 cup freshly grated Parmesan cheese

1. Bring a large pot of salted water to a boil. Add pasta, and cook according to package directions until al dente. Drain, reserving 1/2 cup of cooking liquid, and set aside.
2. While pasta cooks, heat olive oil in a heavy 12-inch skillet over medium-high heat. Add garlic and red pepper flakes. Reduce heat to low, and cook, stirring constantly, for 1 minute, or until garlic is golden brown.
3. Remove the pan from the heat, and add the pasta. Toss well, adding some reserved cooking liquid if mixture seems dry. Season to taste with salt, and serve immediately, passing Parmesan cheese separately.

> Reserving some of the pasta cooking water is a traditional step in Italian cooking for pastas in relatively dry sauces. It can moisten the sauce with the same innate flavor without making the dish taste "watery."

Rigatoni in Creamy Tomato Sauce

Here is an easy and creamy pasta dish that the whole family will adore. Serve it with a green salad.

Yield: 6–8 servings | **Active time:** 15 minutes | **Start to finish:** 35 minutes

     1 pound rigatoni pasta
     3 tablespoons olive oil
     1 large onion, peeled and diced
     2 celery ribs, rinsed, trimmed, and chopped
     3 garlic cloves, peeled and minced
     1 (8-ounce) can tomato sauce
     1 (14.5-ounce) can diced tomatoes, undrained
     1½ cups heavy cream
     2 tablespoons chopped fresh parsley
     2 teaspoons dried oregano
     1½ teaspoons dried thyme
     Salt and freshly ground black pepper to taste
     ¾ cup freshly grated Parmesan cheese

1. Bring a large pot of salted water to a boil. Add pasta, and cook according to package directions until al dente. Drain, and set aside.
2. While water heats, heat olive oil in a saucepan over medium-high heat. Add onion, celery, and garlic, and cook, stirring frequently, for 3 minutes, or until onion is translucent. Stir in tomato sauce, tomatoes, cream, parsley, oregano, and thyme.
3. Bring to a boil, reduce the heat to low, and simmer sauce, uncovered, stirring occasionally, for 20 minutes. Add pasta to sauce, season to taste with salt and pepper, and serve immediately, passing Parmesan cheese separately.

Note: The sauce can be prepared up to 3 days in advance and refrigerated, tightly covered. Reheat over low heat, stirring occasionally, until simmering. Cook pasta just prior to serving.

Mexican Pasta in Chipotle Sauce

This is one of my favorite spicy ways to make pasta; the combination of the heady spices and creamy cheese in a tomato sauce is just delicious. A salad made with shredded jicama is a good complement to the flavors in the dish.

Yield: 6–8 servings | **Active time:** 15 minutes | **Start to finish:** 35 minutes

> ¼ cup olive oil
> 2 medium onions, peeled and finely chopped
> 4 garlic cloves, peeled and minced
> 1 pound angel hair pasta, broken into 2-inch lengths
> 1 tablespoon smoked Spanish paprika
> 1 tablespoon dried oregano
> 1 teaspoon ground cumin
> 1 (14.5-ounce) can diced tomatoes, drained
> 1 (8-ounce) can tomato sauce
> 2 canned chipotle chiles in adobo sauce, drained and finely chopped
> 2 cups Vegetable Stock (recipe on page 35) or purchased stock
> ½ cup sliced pimiento-stuffed green olives
> 1½ cups grated Monterey Jack cheese
> Salt and freshly ground black pepper to taste

1. Heat oil in a large covered skillet over medium-high heat. Add onions and garlic, and cook, stirring frequently, for 3 minutes, or until onion is translucent. Add pasta, paprika, oregano, and cumin. Cook, stirring constantly, for 2 minutes, or until pasta is lightly browned.

2. Add tomatoes, tomato sauce, chipotle chiles, stock, and olives to the pan, and bring to a boil over high heat, stirring occasionally. Reduce the heat to low, and simmer mixture, covered, for 8–10 minutes, or until pasta is soft and liquid has almost evaporated. Stir in cheese, season to taste with salt and pepper, and serve immediately.

Note: The dish can be prepared up to 2 days in advance and refrigerated, tightly covered. Reheat it, covered, in a 350°F oven for 20–25 minutes, or until hot.

Variation: Try this spicier way to enjoy this dish:
- Substitute jalapeño Jack for the milder cheese.

Toasting pasta, as in this recipe, is a technique used in much of Mexico and Latin America. The toasting keeps the strands much more separate as they cook, and they take longer to cook because the starch on the surface has hardened.

Asian Black Bean "Chili"

This is as hearty a bean dish as you could find in any cuisine; the black beans are enlivened by a wide range of Asian flavors. Serve it over aromatic jasmine rice to form a complete protein.

Yield: 4-6 servings | **Active time:** 15 minutes | **Start to finish:** 2 hours, including 1 hour for beans to soak

> 1½ cups dried black beans
> 2 tablespoons Asian sesame oil*
> 8 scallions, white parts and 3 inches of green tops, rinsed, trimmed, and sliced
> 3 garlic cloves, peeled and minced
> 2 tablespoons grated fresh ginger
> 4 cups Vegetable Stock (recipe on page 35) or purchased stock
> ½ cup dry sherry
> ¼ cup hoisin sauce*
> ¼ cup soy sauce
> 3 tablespoons rice vinegar
> 2 tablespoons Chinese black bean sauce*
> 2 teaspoons Chinese chile paste with garlic*
> 2 teaspoons granulated sugar
> Salt and freshly ground black pepper
> ½ cup chopped fresh cilantro

1. Soak beans in cold water to cover for a minimum of 6 hours, or preferably overnight. Or, place beans in a saucepan covered with water, and bring to a boil over high heat. Boil for 1 minute, turn off the heat, and cover the pan. Allow beans to soak for 1 hour, then drain. With either method, continue with the dish as soon as beans have soaked, or refrigerate beans.

2. Heat sesame oil in a 3-quart saucepan over medium-high heat. Add scallions, garlic, and ginger, and cook for 30 seconds, stirring constantly. Add beans, stock, sherry, hoisin sauce, soy sauce, vinegar, black bean sauce, chile paste, and sugar, and bring to a boil over high heat, stirring occasionally.

* Available in the Asian aisle of most supermarkets and in specialty markets.

3. Reduce the heat to low, and cook mixture, covered, for 45–55 minutes, or until beans are tender. Season to taste with salt and pepper, and stir in cilantro. Serve immediately over rice.

Note: The dish can be made up to 2 days in advance and refrigerated, tightly covered. Reheat it over low heat, covered, until hot, stirring occasionally.

> Proper storage can give extra life to leafy herbs like cilantro, parsley, and dill. Treat them like a bouquet of flowers; trim the stems when you get home from the market and then stand the bunch in a glass of water in the refrigerator.

Tuscan-Style White Beans with Zucchini

This hearty Italian bean dish is loaded with flavor from olives and herbs, and it's also a very pretty dish due to the inclusion of fresh, reasonably priced zucchini. A loaf of crusty bread is a nice addition to the meal.

Yield: 6–8 servings | **Active time:** 15 minutes | **Start to finish:** 50 minutes

    3 tablespoons olive oil, divided
    1 medium onion, peeled and chopped
    2 celery ribs, rinsed, trimmed, and thinly sliced
    4 garlic cloves, peeled and minced, divided
    3 medium zucchini, trimmed, quartered lengthwise, and thinly
      sliced
    1 (28-ounce) can diced tomatoes, drained
    3 (15-ounce) cans small white navy beans, drained and rinsed
    1/3 cup pitted oil-cured black olives, halved
    1 tablespoon Italian seasoning, divided
    Salt and freshly ground black pepper to taste
    1 cup plain breadcrumbs
    1/2 cup freshly grated Parmesan cheese
    1/4 cup chopped fresh parsley

1. Preheat the oven to 350°F, and grease a 9x13-inch baking pan.
2. Heat 2 tablespoons oil in a skillet over medium-high heat. Add onion, celery, and 3 garlic cloves, and cook, stirring frequently, for 3 minutes, or until onion is translucent. Add zucchini, and cook, stirring frequently, for an additional 3 minutes, or until zucchini starts to soften.
3. Remove the skillet from the heat, and stir in tomatoes and beans. Mash about 1/4 of beans with the back of a large spoon or a potato masher. Stir in olives and 2 teaspoons Italian seasoning, and season to taste with salt and pepper. Scrape mixture into the prepared pan.

4. Combine remaining 1 tablespoon olive oil, remaining 1 clove minced garlic, remaining 1 teaspoon Italian seasoning, breadcrumbs, Parmesan, and parsley in a mixing bowl. Mix well. Sprinkle topping over beans, and bake for 35–40 minutes, or until bubbling and top is golden brown. Cool 5 minutes before serving.

Note: The dish can be prepared for baking up to 2 days in advance and refrigerated, tightly covered. Allow it to reach room temperature before baking.

Beans are high in carbohydrates, and this makes them a natural thickener for dishes. That's the purpose of mashing some of the beans for this dish, and the same procedure can be used when cooking any bean dish.

Curried Lentils

Healthful lentils, called dal in Indian cooking, are one of the few dried legumes that need no pre-soaking, so this flavorful dish is on your dinner table quickly. Serve it with a tossed salad.

Yield: 4-6 servings | **Active time:** 15 minutes | **Start to finish:** 55 minutes

¼ cup vegetable oil

2 onions, peeled and chopped

3 garlic cloves, peeled and minced

1 fresh jalapeño or serrano chile, seeds and ribs removed, and finely chopped

1 tablespoon curry powder

1 teaspoon ground cumin

1 teaspoon ground coriander

½ teaspoon ground ginger

2 medium tomatoes, rinsed, cored, seeded, and chopped

1 ½ cups brown lentils, picked over and rinsed well

4 cups Vegetable Stock (recipe on page 35) or purchased stock

2 (3-inch) cinnamon sticks

3 medium zucchini, rinsed, trimmed, and cut into ½-inch dice

¼ cup chopped fresh cilantro

Salt and freshly ground black pepper to taste

3 cups cooked basmati rice, hot

1. Heat oil in a Dutch oven over medium-high heat. Add onions, garlic, and chile, and cook, stirring frequently, for 3 minutes, or until onions are translucent. Stir in curry powder, cumin, coriander, and ginger. Cook, stirring constantly, for 1 minute.

2. Add tomatoes, lentils, stock, and cinnamon sticks to the pan, and bring to a boil over medium-high heat. Reduce the heat to low, and simmer mixture, uncovered, adding more stock, if necessary, to keep ingredients just covered with liquid, for 30–40 minutes, or until lentils are very soft.

3. Remove and discard cinnamon sticks, and add zucchini to the pan. Cover the pan, and cook for 10 minutes, or until zucchini is tender. Stir in cilantro, season to taste with salt and pepper, and serve immediately over rice.

Note: The dish can be cooked up to 2 days in advance and refrigerated, tightly covered. Reheat it over low heat, stirring occasionally.

Hearty Vegetarian Chili

Bulgur, an ancient grain, has a nutty flavor and "meaty" texture after it's cooked. It makes a great addition to this hearty chili, which is delicious served over healthful brown rice.

Yield: 6–8 servings | **Active time:** 15 minutes | **Start to finish:** 35 minutes

2 tablespoons olive oil
1 large onion, peeled and chopped
5 garlic cloves, peeled and minced
2 carrots, peeled and chopped
1 green bell pepper, seeds and ribs removed, and chopped
2 jalapeño or serrano chiles, seeds and ribs removed, and finely chopped
2 tablespoons chili powder
2 teaspoons ground cumin
1 teaspoon dried oregano
1 (28-ounce) can crushed tomatoes in tomato puree
2 cups water
3 (15-ounce) cans kidney beans, drained and rinsed
1/2 cup bulgur
Salt and freshly ground black pepper to taste
1 small onion, peeled and diced
1/2 cup sour cream
1/2 cup grated cheddar cheese

1. Heat oil in a saucepan over medium-high heat. Add onion and garlic, and cook, stirring frequently, for 3 minutes, or until onion is translucent. Add carrots, green pepper, and chiles, and cook for 2 minutes. Add chili powder, cumin, and oregano, and cook for 1 minute, stirring constantly.

2. Add tomatoes, water, beans, and bulgur. Bring to a boil, reduce the heat to medium, and cook, uncovered, for 20 minutes, or until bulgur is tender, stirring occasionally. Season to taste with salt and pepper, and serve immediately on top of rice. Place onion, sour cream, and cheese in bowls, and pass them separately.

Note: The dish can be made up to 2 days in advance and refrigerated, tightly covered. Reheat it, covered, over low heat, stirring occasionally, until hot.

Zucchini Chili

Cubes of tender zucchini take the place of meat or poultry in this authentically seasoned Texas chili, which should be served with a tossed salad. Because it calls for canned beans, it's on the table in minutes.

Yield: 4–6 servings | **Active time:** 15 minutes | **Start to finish:** 35 minutes

1 pound small zucchini

2 tablespoons olive oil

1 large onion, peeled and diced

1/2 green bell pepper, seeds and ribs removed, and chopped

3 garlic cloves, peeled and minced

3 tablespoons chili powder

1 tablespoon ground cumin

2 teaspoons dried oregano

1 (15-ounce) can red kidney beans, drained and rinsed

1 (28-ounce) can crushed tomatoes in tomato puree

1 (4-ounce) can diced mild green chiles, drained

2 tablespoons tomato paste

1 tablespoon granulated sugar

Salt and cayenne to taste

3 cups cooked rice, hot

1. Rinse and trim zucchini. Cut zucchini lengthwise into quarters and then into 1/2-inch slices. Soak zucchini in a bowl of salted cold water for 10 minutes. Drain, and set aside.

2. While zucchini soaks, heat oil in a medium saucepan over medium-high heat. Add onion, green bell pepper, and garlic, and cook, stirring frequently, for 3 minutes, or until onion is translucent. Reduce the heat to low, and stir in chili powder, cumin, and oregano. Cook for 1 minute, stirring constantly.

3. Add zucchini, kidney beans, tomatoes, green chiles, tomato paste, and sugar to the pan, and bring to a boil over medium-high heat, stirring occasionally. Reduce the heat to low, and cook, stirring occasionally, for 15 minutes, or until zucchini is tender. Season to taste with salt and cayenne, and serve immediately over rice.

Note: The dish can be made up to 2 days in advance and refrigerated, tightly covered. Reheat it over low heat, covered, until hot, stirring occasionally.

Variations: Have other vegetables in the house? Try these:

- Substitute yellow squash, and prepare it exactly like the zucchini.
- Substitute thinly sliced carrots for the zucchini; they will not need soaking but will cook in the same amount of time.

While soaking the zucchini is salted water is a step that can be skipped if time is at a premium, I think you'll like the results of this recipe better if you take the time. Salting draws some of the liquid out of the fibers of the vegetable so that it retains texture better once cooked. It's a trick I picked up from traditional Mediterranean cooking.

Southwest Spinach Loaf

This loaf, made with reasonably priced frozen spinach, is both flavorful and light. It contains a few different types of cheese, and crushed tortilla chips add an appealing textural contrast.

Yield: 6–8 servings | **Active time:** 10 minutes | **Start to finish:** 1¼ hours

    4 large eggs
    2 (10-ounce) packages frozen chopped spinach, thawed
    1½ cups tortilla chips, divided
    1 cup grated jalapeño Jack cheese
    ½ cup freshly grated Parmesan cheese
    ½ cup cottage cheese
    3 scallions, white parts and 2 inches of green tops, rinsed, trimmed,
        and thinly sliced
    ½ cup breadcrumbs
    3 tablespoons heavy cream
    1 tablespoon ground cumin
    1 teaspoon dried oregano
    Salt and freshly ground black pepper to taste

1. Preheat the oven to 350°F, and grease a 2-quart soufflé dish. Bring a kettle of water to a boil over high heat.
2. Whisk eggs in a large mixing bowl. Place spinach in a colander, and press with the back of a spoon to extract as much liquid as possible. Add spinach to the mixing bowl. Place corn tortilla chips in a heavy plastic bag, and pound with the flat side of meat mallet or the bottom of small skillet until coarse crumbs form. Add ½ of crumbs to the mixing bowl.
3. Add jalapeño Jack cheese, Parmesan cheese, cottage cheese, scallions, breadcrumbs, cream, cumin, oregano, salt, and pepper to the mixing bowl. Stir well. Scrape mixture into the prepared soufflé dish, and smooth top with a rubber spatula. Sprinkle with remaining corn chip crumbs, and cover the pan lightly with foil.

4. Place the soufflé dish in large roasting pan, and pour boiling water into roasting pan to come halfway up sides of the soufflé dish. Bake for 20 minutes. Remove the foil, and bake for an additional 40 minutes, or until a skewer inserted in the center comes out clean. Remove the soufflé dish from the roasting pan, and serve immediately.

Note: The dish can be prepared for baking up to 1 day in advance and refrigerated, tightly covered. Add 10 minutes to the covered baking time if chilled.

Variations: Not fond of spinach? Try this:
- Substitute frozen chopped broccoli for the spinach.
- For a milder dish, substitute Monterey Jack cheese for the spicier version.

While cooking is primarily an art, science enters the picture, too. The reason to surround the soufflé dish with the boiling water is to keep the eggs from turning tough. It's true that you can cook an egg on a hot sidewalk; eggs actually begin to cook at less than the 212°F that it takes to boil water. The water bath keeps the eggs tender.

Mexican Spaghetti Squash au Gratin

Spaghetti squash, which are shaped like small watermelons, get their name from the fact that once cooked, the flesh can be separated into strands with the tines of a fork. While you can enjoy this vegetable with any Italian pasta sauce, I like it equally well with these Hispanic flavors.

Yield: 6–8 servings | **Active time:** 15 minutes | **Start to finish:** 1 ½ hours

- 1 medium (3-pound) spaghetti squash
- 2 tablespoons olive oil
- 1 medium red onion, peeled and chopped
- 2 garlic cloves, peeled and minced
- 1 jalapeño or serrano chile, seeds and ribs removed, and finely chopped
- 2 teaspoons dried oregano
- 1 teaspoon ground cumin
- 1 (14.5-ounce) can diced tomatoes, undrained
- 1 (8-ounce) can tomato sauce
- 1 (4-ounce) can diced mild green chiles, drained
- 1 teaspoon granulated sugar
- 1 teaspoon cider vinegar
- Salt and freshly ground black pepper to taste
- 1 cup grated Monterey Jack cheese

1. Preheat the oven to 375°F, and grease a 9x13-inch baking pan. Pierce squash with a meat fork in several places, and place it on a baking sheet. Bake for 45–55 minutes, turning once during baking, or until skin of squash yields to pressure when pressed. Remove squash from the oven.

2. While squash bakes, heat oil in saucepan over medium-high heat. Add onion, garlic, and chile, and cook, stirring frequently, for 3 minutes, or until onion is translucent. Add oregano and cumin, and cook, stirring constantly, for 1 minute.

3. Add tomatoes, tomato sauce, green chiles, sugar, and vinegar to the pan, and bring to a boil. Reduce the heat to low, and simmer sauce, partially covered, for 20 minutes, stirring occasionally. Turn off the heat, and set aside.

4. When squash is cool enough to handle, slice in half lengthwise, and discard seeds and membranes. Remove squash from shell by combing halves lengthwise with the tines of a fork. Place squash in prepared pan, and stir in sauce. Season to taste with salt and pepper, and sprinkle with cheese.

5. Bake for 25–30 minutes, or until cheese is melted and top is lightly browned. Serve immediately.

Note: The dish can be prepared for baking up to 2 days in advance and refrigerated, tightly covered. Allow it to reach room temperature before baking.

Variations: Here are some ways to vary this dish:

- While spaghetti squash has a rather hard shell, its delicate flavor is more similar to zucchini and yellow squash than to winter squash such as acorn or butternut. You can quickly sauté zucchini or yellow squash instead of taking the time to bake the spaghetti squash.
- To make the dish more Italian than Mexican, use Herbed Tomato Sauce (recipe on page 25) and substitute mozzarella cheese for the Monterey Jack.

Oven-Baked Vegetarian Risotto

Colorful Swiss chard, meaty garbanzo beans, and cheese flavor this rice dish. While an authentic risotto is the result of expending a lot of time stirring the dish on the stove, this baked version is just as delicious—and far less work.

Yield: 6–8 servings | **Active time:** 15 minutes | **Start to finish:** 50 minutes

3 tablespoons unsalted butter
1 medium onion, peeled and chopped
2 garlic cloves, peeled and minced
1½ cups Arborio rice
½ cup dry white wine
3½ cups Vegetable Stock (recipe on page 35) or purchased stock
1 (15-ounce) can garbanzo beans, drained and rinsed
1 (1-pound) bunch Swiss chard, rinsed, stemmed, and chopped
½ cup freshly grated Parmesan cheese
Salt and freshly ground black pepper to taste

1. Preheat the oven to 400°F, and grease a 9x13-inch baking pan.
2. Heat butter in a skillet over medium-high heat. Add onion and garlic and cook, stirring frequently, for 3 minutes, or until onion is translucent. Add rice to pan, and cook for 2 minutes, stirring constantly.
3. Add wine to the skillet, raise the heat to high, and cook for 3 minutes, stirring constantly, or until wine is almost evaporated. Add stock to the skillet, and bring to a boil.
4. Scrape mixture into the prepared pan, cover the pan with aluminum foil, and bake for 15 minutes. Stir in beans and Swiss chard, cover the pan again, and bake for 15–20 minutes, or until rice is soft and has absorbed liquid. Stir in Parmesan cheese, season to taste with salt and pepper, and serve immediately.

Note: The dish can be prepared up to 2 days in advance and refrigerated, tightly covered. Reheat it, covered, in a 350°F oven for 20–25 minutes, or until hot.

Risotto-Style Barley with Spinach

Barley becomes as creamy as Arborio rice when cooked in stock, and the addition of licorice-flavored fresh fennel and lusty spinach add to the dish as well.

Yield: 6–8 servings | **Active time:** 15 minutes | **Start to finish:** 55 minutes

> 1 medium fennel bulb
> 3 tablespoons olive oil
> 1 large onion, peeled and diced
> 1 teaspoon dried thyme
> 2 cups pearl barley, rinsed well
> 6 1/2 cups Vegetable Stock (recipe on page 35) or purchased stock
> 1 (10-ounce) package frozen chopped spinach, thawed and squeezed dry
> 1/2 cup freshly grated Parmesan cheese
> Salt and freshly ground black pepper to taste

1. Trim stalks and root end from fennel bulb. Cut bulb in half, and discard core. Dice fennel, and set aside.
2. Heat oil in a large saucepan over medium-high heat. Add fennel and onion, and cook, stirring frequently, for 3 minutes, or until onion is translucent. Stir in thyme, barley, and stock, and bring to a boil over high heat, stirring occasionally.
3. Reduce the heat to low, and cook, covered, until barley is tender and mixture is creamy, stirring often, about 40 minutes. Add spinach for the last 10 minutes of the cooking time. Stir in Parmesan cheese, season to taste with salt and pepper, and serve immediately.

Note: The dish can be prepared up to 2 days in advance and refrigerated, tightly covered. Reheat it, covered, in a 350°F oven for 20–25 minutes, or until hot.

While the stalks from fennel are not used in recipes calling for fennel bulbs, don't throw them out! They become a crispy addition to salads in place of celery, or can be added to flavor a stock.

Southwestern Squash and Bean Stew

While dried beans frequently require different cooking times, all canned beans are totally cooked and can be combined in dishes such as this one. This is an incredibly flavorful dish, partially due to the fresh salsa in the sauce.

Yield: 4–6 servings | **Active time:** 15 minutes | **Start to finish:** 35 minutes

    3 tablespoons olive oil
    1 large onion, peeled and diced
    3 garlic cloves, peeled and minced
    1 green bell pepper, seeds and ribs removed, and finely chopped
    2 tablespoons chili powder
    1 teaspoon ground cumin
    1 teaspoon dried oregano
    1 (15-ounce) can tomato sauce
    ³/₄ cup purchased refrigerated salsa
    ³/₄ cup Vegetable Stock (recipe on page 35) or purchased stock
    2 medium yellow squash, rinsed, trimmed, and cut into ¹/₂-inch dice
    1 (15-ounce) can red kidney beans, drained and rinsed
    1 (15-ounce) can garbanzo beans, drained and rinsed
    Salt and freshly ground black pepper
    3 cups cooked brown rice, hot

1. Heat olive oil in a medium saucepan over medium-high heat. Add onion, garlic, and green bell pepper, and cook, stirring frequently, for 3 minutes, or until onion is translucent. Stir in chili powder, cumin, and oregano. Cook for 1 minute, stirring constantly.

2. Stir in tomato sauce, salsa, stock, yellow squash, kidney beans, and garbanzo beans, and bring to a boil. Reduce the heat to low and simmer, uncovered, for 20 minutes, or until zucchini is tender. Season to taste with salt and pepper, and serve immediately over rice.

Note: The dish can be made up to 2 days in advance and refrigerated, tightly covered. Reheat it over low heat, covered, until hot, stirring occasionally.

Mediterranean Pizza

A mixture of colorful, healthful vegetables and a few cheeses make this vegetarian pizza a real treat. Serve it with a tossed salad to add textural interest.

Yield: 4 (8-inch) pizzas | **Active time:** 15 minutes | **Start to finish:** 25 minutes

  3 tablespoons olive oil
  1 shallot, peeled and minced
  2 garlic cloves, peeled and minced
  1/4 pound mushrooms, wiped with a damp paper towel, trimmed, and sliced
  1 red bell pepper, seeds and ribs removed, and sliced
  Salt and freshly ground black pepper to taste
  3 tablespoons chopped fresh parsley
  1 recipe Basic Pizza Dough (recipe on page 220) or purchased pizza dough
  1/4 cup yellow cornmeal
  1 cup grated whole-milk mozzarella cheese
  1/2 cup crumbled feta cheese
  1/2 cup sliced Kalamata olives

1. Preheat the oven to 500°F, and move the oven rack to the lowest level.
2. Heat oil in a large skillet over medium-high heat. Add shallot, garlic, mushrooms, and bell pepper. Cook, stirring frequently, for 3 minutes, or until shallot is translucent. Season to taste with salt and pepper, and cook for an additional 5 minutes, or until mushrooms brown and vegetables soften. Stir parsley into mixture.
3. Form pizza dough into 4 (8-inch) circles. Sprinkle cornmeal on a baking sheet, and arrange crusts on top of cornmeal.
4. Divide vegetable mixture on top of dough, stopping 1/2 inch from the edge. Sprinkle mozzarella, feta, and olives on top of vegetables.
5. Bake pizzas for 10–12 minutes, or until crust is golden and crisp. Remove pizzas from the oven, and serve immediately.

Variations: This recipe can be changed in myriad ways:
- Substitute chopped fresh basil or oregano for the parsley.
- Use any color bell pepper you like, or is on sale.

Italian Vegetable Frittata

This frittata—essentially a baked omelet—is really a whole meal, with all important parts of the pyramid represented because there's some pasta in with the eggs and vegetables. It makes a wonderful brunch as well as dinner dish, and you can top it with tomato sauce.

Yield: 4-6 servings | **Active time:** 20 minutes | **Start to finish:** 45 minutes

- ½ cup orzo
- 3 tablespoons olive oil
- 2 small zucchini, rinsed, trimmed, halved lengthwise, and thinly sliced
- 1 small onion, peeled and diced
- 1 garlic clove, peeled and minced
- 2 medium ripe tomatoes, rinsed, cored, seeded, and finely chopped
- 2 tablespoons chopped fresh parsley
- 2 teaspoons Italian seasoning
- Salt and freshly ground black pepper to taste
- 8 large eggs
- ½ cup grated mozzarella cheese
- ¼ cup freshly grated Parmesan cheese
- 2 tablespoons unsalted butter

1. Bring a large pot of salted water to a boil. Cook pasta according to package directions until al dente. Drain, and run under cold water to cool. Set aside.

2. While pasta cooks, heat oil in large skillet over medium-high heat. Add zucchini, onion, and garlic. Cook, stirring frequently, for 3 minutes, or until zucchini is tender. Add tomatoes, parsley, and Italian seasoning. Cook mixture for 5 minutes, or until liquid from tomatoes evaporates, stirring occasionally. Season to taste with salt and pepper, and allow mixture to cool for 10 minutes.

3. Preheat the oven to 425°F. Whisk eggs well, stir in mozzarella and Parmesan cheeses. Stir cooled vegetable mixture into eggs. Heat butter in a large, oven-proof skillet over medium heat. Add egg mixture and cook for 4 minutes, or until the bottom of cake is lightly brown. Transfer the skillet to the oven, and bake for 10–15 minutes, or until top is browned.

4. Run a spatula around the sides of the skillet and under the bottom of the cake to release it. Slide cake gently onto a serving platter, and cut it into wedges. Serve immediately or at room temperature.

Note: The vegetable mixture can be cooked up to 1 day in advance and refrigerated, tightly covered. Reheat the vegetables to room temperature in a microwave-safe dish, or over low heat, before completing the dish.

If you're not sure how fresh your eggs are, place them in a mixing bowl filled with cold water. As eggs age, they develop air pockets, so older eggs float while fresher ones sink.

Chapter 8:
Bakery Basics

While the cost of flour is rising, it's not rising half as fast as the price of foods made with it—from that loaf of white bread to the pizza you have delivered to anything and everything from the bakery aisle. In this chapter you'll learn how easy it is to make these foods at home, and you'll get a sense of how much money you're saving by doing so.

The price of a single muffin is higher at the supermarket than the cost of making a dozen muffins at home, where you can make them with top-quality ingredients. Enough focaccia to feed a crowd costs a fraction of what a boutique bakery charges for a small square, and dozens of tiny cream puffs to fill as profiteroles are virtually pennies each.

PROCEDURAL MATTERS

While cooking is a form of art, when it comes to baking, science class enters the equation as well. These are general pointers on procedures to be used for all genres of baked goods:

- **Measure accurately.** Measure dry ingredients in dry measuring cups, which are plastic or metal, and come in sizes of $1/4$, $1/3$, $1/2$, and 1 cup. Spoon dry ingredients from the container or canister into the measuring cup, and then sweep the top with a straight edge such as the back of a knife or a spatula to measure it properly. Do not dip the cup into the canister or tap it on the counter to produce a level surface. These methods pack down the dry ingredients, and can increase the actual volume by up to 10 percent. Tablespoons and teaspoons should also be leveled; a rounded $1/2$ teaspoon can actually measure almost 1 teaspoon. If the box or can does not have a straight edge built in, then level the excess back into the container with the back of a knife. Measure liquids in liquid measures, which come in various sizes, but are transparent glass or plastic and have lines on the sides. To accurately measure liquids, place the measuring cup on a flat counter, and bend down to read the marked level.

- **Create consistent temperature.** All ingredients should be at room temperature unless otherwise indicated. Having all ingredients at the same temperature makes it easier to combine them into a smooth, homogeneous mixture. Adding cold liquid to a dough or batter can cause the batter to lose its unified structure by making the fat rigid.

- **Preheat the oven.** Some ovens can take up to 25 minutes to reach a high temperature, such as 450°F. The minimum heating time should be 15 minutes.

- **Plan ahead.** Read the recipe thoroughly, and assemble all your ingredients. This means that you have accounted for all ingredients required for a recipe in advance, so you don't get to a step and realize you must improvise. Assembling in advance also lessens the risk of over-mixing dough or batters, as the mixer drones on while you search for spice or a bag of chips.

MARVELOUS MUFFINS AND EASY QUICK BREADS

Muffins and quick breads are being discussed together because the batters are identical in preparation and they're interchangeable; the only difference is the amount of time and at what temperature they are baked.

Quick breads are so named since they are made with a chemical leavening agent, thus eliminating the time spent waiting for yeast dough to rise. Quick breads can be served as an alternative not only to yeast-raised breads, but also in place of potatoes or rice as a base for stews or other braised dishes. Leftover muffins can be used to create a bread pudding, and leftover quick bread can be turned into a wonderful French toast or stuffing (by first toasting the cubes).

Baked Goods	Time	Temperature
Standard Muffins	18–22 minutes	400°F
Oversized Muffins	20–25 minutes	375°F
Quick Breads	45 minutes–1 hour	350°F

YEASTY MATTERS

Many cooks are afraid of working with yeast, so they do not consider making yeast-risen breads or pizza crust at home. But the whole process could not be easier, and this section provides a primer on how to work with this live leavening agent.

All bread depends on the interaction of some sort of flour, liquid, and leavening agent. Wheat flour contains many substances, including protein, starch, lipids, sugars, and enzymes. When the proteins combine with water, they form gluten. Gluten is both plastic and elastic. This quality means that it will hold the carbon dioxide produced by the yeast, but will not allow it to escape or break. It is this plasticity that allows bread to rise before it is baked, at which time the structure of the dough solidifies due to the heat.

There are two types of yeast—dry (or granulated) yeast and fresh (or compressed) yeast. Yeast is an organic leavening agent, which means that it must be alive in order to be effective. The yeast can be killed by overly high temperatures and, conversely, cold temperatures can inhibit the yeast's action. That is why dry yeast should be refrigerated. It will keep for several months, while fresh yeast is quite perishable and can be held under refrigeration for only seven to ten days. The fast-rising yeasts are all dry, and they do cut back on the time needed for rising.

To make sure your yeast is alive, you should start by a step called "proofing." Combine the yeast with warm liquid (100–110°F) and a small amount of flour or sugar. If the water is any hotter, it might kill the yeast. Either use a meat thermometer to take the temperature, or make sure it feels warm but not hot on the underside of your wrist.

Let the mixture rest at room temperature for five minutes until a thick surface foam forms, which indicates that the yeast is alive and can be used. If there is no foam, the yeast is dead and should be discarded. After your proofing is successful, you are ready to make the dough.

Basic Muffins

Once you see how easy muffins are to make you'll never spend money again to bring them in from a bakery. This recipe is for a basic muffin that's slightly sweet, and perfect to top with butter and jam. Following the recipe are some of the hundreds of variations you can make.

Yield: 12 muffins | **Active time:** 10 minutes | **Start to finish:** 30 minutes

> 2 cups all-purpose flour
> 3 tablespoons granulated sugar
> 1 tablespoon baking powder
> 1/2 teaspoon salt
> 1 cup whole milk
> 1 large egg, beaten
> 5 tablespoons unsalted butter, melted
> 1/2 teaspoon pure vanilla extract

1. Preheat the oven to 400°F, and grease a 12-cup muffin pan.
2. Combine flour, sugar, baking powder, and salt in a large mixing bowl, and whisk well. Add milk, egg, butter, and vanilla. Stir gently to wet flour, but do not whisk until smooth; batter should be lumpy. Fill each prepared cup 2/3 full.
3. Bake muffins for 18–20 minutes, or until a toothpick inserted in the center comes out clean. Place muffin pan on a cooling rack for 10 minutes, then serve.

Note: Muffins can be served hot or at room temperature.

Variations: Now that you can do the basics, it's time for improvisation:
- For blueberry muffins, mix 1/4 cup of the flour with 1 cup fresh or dry-packed frozen blueberries, and increase the sugar to 1/2 cup. Add blueberries to the batter last. You can also add 2 teaspoons grated lemon zest and omit vanilla.
- For nut muffins, toast 3/4 cup chopped pecans, walnuts, or hazelnuts in the preheated oven for 3–5 minutes, or until browned. Increase the sugar to 1/2 cup, and mix all but 2 tablespoons sugar and 1/2 cup nuts into batter. Combine remaining nuts, remaining sugar, and 1/4 teaspoon ground cinnamon in a small bowl. Sprinkle mixture on top of batter before baking muffins.
- For dried fruit muffins, add 1/2 cup chopped dates, raisins, currants, dried cranberries, or some combination of dried fruit.
- For whole wheat muffins, use a combination of 1 cup all-purpose flour and 3/4 cup whole wheat flour. Add 1/4 cup toasted wheat germ, and increase sugar to 1/4 cup.

Bran Apple Muffins

The rehydrated apples add moisture as well as flavor to this easy muffin batter, and eating a few muffins significantly increases your daily fiber intake.

Yield: 12 muffins | **Active time:** 15 minutes | **Start to finish:** 35 minutes

1 cup toasted wheat bran

½ cup chopped dried apples

½ cup boiling water

¼ cup honey

1¼ cups all-purpose flour

⅓ cup firmly packed light brown sugar

2 teaspoons baking soda

½ teaspoons salt

½ teaspoon ground cinnamon

1 cup buttermilk, shaken well

5 tablespoons unsalted butter, melted

1 large egg, beaten

¼ teaspoon pure vanilla extract

1. Preheat the oven to 400°F, and grease a 12-cup muffin pan; you can also use paper liners.
2. Combine wheat bran, dried apples, boiling water, and honey in a small bowl, and stir well. Allow mixture to sit for 5 minutes.
3. Combine flour, sugar, baking soda, salt, and cinnamon in a large mixing bowl, and whisk well. Combine buttermilk, butter, egg, vanilla, and bran mixture in another bowl, and whisk well. Stir liquid mixture into dry mixture gently to wet flour, but do not whisk until smooth; batter should be lumpy. Fill each prepared cup ⅔ full.
4. Bake muffins for 18–20 minutes, or until a toothpick inserted in the center comes out clean. Place muffin pan on a cooling rack for 10 minutes, then serve.

Note: Muffins can be served hot or at room temperature.

Variations: Here are some ways to personalize this recipe:
- Add ½ cup chopped toasted nuts to batter.
- Substitute raisins, dried cranberries, dried currants, or chopped dried dates or figs for dried apples.

Parmesan Herb Muffins

Savory muffins can replace expensive breads on your dinner table, and because no yeast is used they can be on the table quickly.

Yield: 12 muffins | **Active time:** 10 minutes | **Start to finish:** 30 minutes

1½ cups all-purpose flour
2 teaspoons baking powder
2 teaspoons Italian seasoning
½ teaspoon baking soda
½ teaspoon salt
Freshly ground black pepper to taste
¾ cup whole milk
2 large eggs, beaten
½ cup olive oil
3 tablespoons chopped fresh parsley
1 cup freshly grated Parmesan cheese, divided
2 garlic cloves, peeled and minced

1. Preheat the oven to 400°F, and grease a 12-cup muffin pan; you can also use paper liners.
2. Combine flour, baking powder, Italian seasoning, baking soda, salt, and pepper in a large mixing bowl, and whisk well. Add milk, eggs, oil, parsley, ⅔ cup cheese, and garlic. Stir gently to wet flour, but do not whisk until smooth; batter should be lumpy. Fill each prepared cup ⅔ full, and sprinkle with remaining cheese.
3. Bake muffins for 18–20 minutes, or until a toothpick inserted in the center comes out clean. Place muffin pan on a cooling rack for 10 minutes, then serve.

Note: Muffins can be served hot or at room temperature.

Variations: Parmesan is a wonderful flavor for muffins, and here are some additions you can make:

- Add ½ cup sun-dried tomatoes packed in olive oil, drained and chopped. Use the olive oil from the tomatoes as part of the oil for the recipe.
- Substitute dried oregano for the Italian seasoning, and add 1 tablespoon grated lemon zest.

Basic Beer Bread

I love beer bread because it has the same yeasty aroma and flavor as a rustic yeast bread, but it's so easy to make. In addition to serving it at dinner, I use it in place of sandwich bread.

Yield: 1 loaf | **Active time:** 10 minutes | **Start to finish:** 50 minutes

3½ cups all-purpose flour
1 teaspoon baking powder
½ teaspoon salt
½ teaspoon baking soda
1 large egg, beaten lightly
1 (12-ounce) can lager beer

1. Preheat the oven to 350°F, and grease a 9x5x3-inch loaf pan.
2. Combine flour, baking powder, salt, and baking soda in a large mixing bowl, and whisk well. Add egg and beer, and stir until batter is just combined; batter should be lumpy. Scrape batter into the prepared pan.
3. Bake bread for 40–45 minutes, or until a toothpick inserted in the center comes out clean. Place pan on a cooling rack for 5 minutes, then turn bread out of the pan and serve.

Note: Bread can be served hot or at room temperature.

Variations: Here are some ways to add extra flavor to this recipe:
- For a sweeter bread, add ½ cup granulated sugar.
- Add ½ cup chopped sun-dried tomatoes or ½ cup chopped oil-cured black olives, or ¼ cup of each.
- Add ½ cup chopped scallions, white parts and 3 inches of green tops.
- Add ¼ cup chopped fresh dill.

Kneading is the process of working dough to make it pliable, so it will hold the gas bubbles from the leavening agent and expand when heated. It is is done with a pressing-folding-turning action. Press down into the dough with the heels of both hands, then push your hands away from your body. Fold the dough in half, and give it a quarter turn; then repeat the process.

Irish Soda Bread

This hearty and rustic bread is one of the easiest to make, and it comes to the table looking pretty with a bright, shiny crust.

Yield: 2 (6-inch) loaves | **Active time:** 10 minutes | **Start to finish:** 50 minutes

> 4 cups all-purpose flour
> 2 tablespoons granulated sugar
> 1½ teaspoons baking soda
> 1 teaspoon salt
> 1¾ cups buttermilk, shaken well
> 2 tablespoons unsalted butter, melted

1. Preheat the oven to 375°F, and grease and flour a baking sheet.
2. Combine flour, sugar, baking soda, and salt in a large mixing bowl, and whisk well. Add buttermilk, and stir until batter is just combined; batter should be lumpy. Transfer dough to a well-floured surface, and knead with floured hands for 1 minute, or until dough is less sticky.
3. Divide dough in half, and pat each half into a 6-inch round on the prepared baking sheet. Cut an X that is ½ inch deep on top of each round, and brush tops with butter.
4. Bake bread for 35–40 minutes, or until tops are golden. Transfer loaves to a cooling rack with a wide spatula, and cool for at least 15 minutes.

Note: The bread can be served the day it is made, but it slices more easily if kept, wrapped in plastic wrap, at room temperature for 1 day, and up to 4 days.

Variations: Soda bread is a blank canvas on which to experiment:
- Add 1 cup raisins to dough, or 1 cup any chopped dried fruit like dried apples or pitted dates.
- Add ½ cup chopped scallions, white parts and 3 inches of green tops
- Add 2 tablespoons crushed caraway seeds or fennel seeds

Whole Wheat Oatmeal Soda Bread

Here's a variation on soda bread that adds heart-healthy grains to your diet as well as their innate flavors and aromas to the bread.

Yield: 2 (7-inch) loaves | **Active time:** 10 minutes | **Start to finish:** 50 minutes

2¼ cups all-purpose flour

2 cups whole-wheat flour

1¼ cups old-fashioned rolled oats, divided

2 teaspoons baking soda

1 teaspoon baking powder

½ teaspoon salt

2 cups buttermilk

1 large egg, beaten

2 tablespoons unsalted butter, melted

1. Preheat the oven to 375°F, and grease and flour a baking sheet.
2. Combine all-purpose flour, whole-wheat flour, 1 cup oats, baking soda, baking powder, and salt in a large mixing bowl, and whisk well. Add buttermilk and egg, and stir until batter is just combined; batter should be lumpy. Transfer dough to a well-floured surface, and knead with floured hands for 1 minute, or until dough is less sticky.
3. Divide dough in half, and pat each half into a 7-inch round on the prepared baking sheet. Cut an X that is ½ inch deep on top of each round, and brush tops with butter. Sprinkle loaves with remaining oats.
4. Bake bread for 35–40 minutes, or until tops are golden. Transfer loaves to a cooling rack with a wide spatula, and cool for at least 15 minutes.

Note: The bread can be served the day it is made, but it slices more easily if kept, wrapped in plastic wrap, at room temperature for 1 day, and up to 4 days.

Basic Herb Quick Bread

In addition to being a delicious accompaniment to any meal, this loaf also can be transformed into savory French toast for a brunch; top it with a marinara sauce.

Yield: 1 loaf | **Active time:** 10 minutes | **Start to finish:** 1 hour

3 cups all-purpose flour
2 tablespoons granulated sugar
2 tablespoons baking powder
2 tablespoons herbes de Provence
1 teaspoon salt
Freshly ground black pepper to taste
2 large eggs, beaten
1¼ cups whole milk
⅓ cup olive oil

1. Preheat the oven to 350°F, and grease a 9x5x3-inch loaf pan.
2. Combine flour, sugar, baking powder, herbes de Provence, salt, and pepper in a large mixing bowl, and whisk well. Add eggs, milk, and oil, and stir until batter is just combined; batter should be lumpy. Scrape batter into the prepared pan.
3. Bake bread for 50–55 minutes, or until a toothpick inserted in the center comes out clean. Place pan on a cooling rack for 10 minutes, then turn bread out of the pan and serve.

Note: Bread can be served hot or at room temperature.

Variations: Here are other ways to flavor this loaf:
- Substitute Italian seasoning for the herbes de Provence for an equally complex but more assertive flavor.
- Add 3 tablespoons chopped fresh parsley.
- Omit the herbs and add ¼ cup chopped oil-cured black olives.

Sun-Dried Tomato Herb Quick Bread

This aromatic, flavorful quick bread makes a wonderful grilled cheese sandwich if sliced thin and toasted with some fontina or mozzarella cheese in the center.

Yield: 1 loaf | **Active time:** 10 minutes | **Start to finish:** 1 hour

2 cups all-purpose flour
1 tablespoon baking powder
1/2 teaspoon salt
1/4 teaspoon freshly ground pepper
1 cup whole milk
1/3 cup olive oil
1 large egg, beaten
1/2 cup freshly grated Parmesan cheese
1/4 cup finely chopped sun-dried tomato packed in oil
2 tablespoons chopped fresh parsley
1 tablespoon chopped fresh herbs (oregano, basil, marjoram, or a combination)

1. Preheat the oven to 350°F, and grease a 9x5x3-inch loaf pan.
2. Combine flour, baking powder, salt, and pepper in a large mixing bowl, and whisk well. Add milk, oil, egg, cheese, sun-dried tomatoes, parsley, and herbs, and stir until batter is just combined; batter should be lumpy. Scrape batter into the prepared pan.
3. Bake bread for 50–55 minutes, or until a toothpick inserted in the center comes out clean. Place pan on a cooling rack for 10 minutes, then turn bread out of the pan and serve.

Note: Bread can be served hot or at room temperature.

Banana Bread

Rum enhances the natural sweetness of bananas in this bread, which is densely textured and rich. For a special treat, beat some orange zest and honey into softened butter to serve as a topping.

Yield: 1 loaf | **Active time:** 10 minutes | **Start to finish:** 1 hour

½ cup firmly packed dark brown sugar
¼ cup granulated sugar
5 tablespoons unsalted butter, softened
1 large egg
3 large ripe bananas, peeled and mashed
2 tablespoons dark rum
½ teaspoon pure vanilla extract
2 cups all-purpose flour
1 teaspoon baking soda
1 teaspoon baking powder
¼ teaspoon salt

1. Preheat the oven to 350°F, and grease a 9x5x3-inch loaf pan.
2. Combine brown sugar, granulated sugar, and butter in a mixing bowl, and beat at medium speed with an electric mixer until light and fluffy. Add egg, bananas, rum, and vanilla, and beat until smooth.
3. Combine flour, baking soda, baking powder, and salt , and lightly beat into banana mixture.
4. Scrape batter into the prepared pan, and bake in the center of the oven for 50–55 minutes, or until a toothpick inserted in the center comes out clean. Allow bread to sit for 5 minutes, then remove it from the pan, and cool it completely on a rack.

Note: The bread can be made up to 2 days in advance, and kept tightly covered with plastic wrap once cooled. It can be frozen for up to 2 months.

If you have bananas that are getting overly ripe, don't throw them out and waste the money. Instead, freeze them right in the peels. When ready to make banana bread or a smoothie, take out the banana and allow it to thaw.

Buttermilk Biscuits

A true Southern biscuit is a tender, flaky work of art that is incredibly easy to make, and once you have made a batch you will become addicted!

Yield: 20 (2-inch) biscuits | **Active time:** 10 minutes | **Start to finish:** 30 minutes

1½ cups cake flour *(not self-rising)*
½ cup all-purpose flour
1 tablespoon baking powder
½ teaspoon salt
½ teaspoon baking soda
6 tablespoons vegetable shortening, such as Crisco
⅔ cup buttermilk
3 tablespoons unsalted butter, melted

1. Preheat oven to 425°F, and lightly grease a baking sheet.
2. Sift cake flour, all-purpose flour, baking powder, salt, and baking soda into a large mixing bowl. Cut in the vegetable shortening using a pastry blender, two knives, or your fingertips until mixture resembles coarse meal. Add buttermilk, and stir with a fork until just combined.
3. Transfer mixture to a lightly floured surface, and knead 10 times with the heel of your hand to bring the dough together. Pat dough into a round that is ½ inch thick.
4. Cut dough into 2-inch circles and place them 1 inch apart on the prepared baking sheet. Brush tops with melted butter. Gather scraps and pat into a circle again to cut out more biscuits. Repeat until all dough is used.
5. Bake for 18–20 minutes, or until cooked through and golden brown. Serve immediately.

Note: The biscuits can be cut out up to 1 hour in advance. Do not bake them until just prior to serving.

Variations: Here are some ways to dress up these homey treats:
- For cheese biscuits, add ½ cup grated cheddar, Swiss, or Gruyère cheese to the dough.
- For breakfast biscuits, combine ⅓ cup firmly packed dark brown sugar, ½ cup toasted chopped nuts, and ½ teaspoon ground cinnamon in a small bowl, and pat the mixture onto the top of biscuits before baking.

Cornbread

If you have a well-seasoned cast iron skillet around, you can bake the cornbread right in it, and then bring it to the table. This is an all-purpose recipe that really goes with any entree and is as at home on the breakfast table as on the dinner table.

Yield: 6–8 servings | **Active time:** 10 minutes | **Start to finish:** 30 minutes

1 cup yellow cornmeal
1 cup all-purpose flour
2 tablespoons granulated sugar
1½ teaspoons baking powder
½ teaspoon baking soda
¼ teaspoon salt
2 large eggs
¾ cups buttermilk, well shaken
½ cup creamed corn
5 tablespoons unsalted butter, melted

1. Preheat the oven to 425°F, and grease a 9-inch-square pan or cast iron skillet generously.
2. Whisk together cornmeal, flour, sugar, baking powder, baking soda, and salt in a large mixing bowl. Whisk together eggs, buttermilk, creamed corn, and butter in a small bowl. Add buttermilk mixture to cornmeal mixture, and stir batter until just blended.
3. Heat the greased pan in the oven for 3 minutes, or until it is very hot. Remove the pan from the oven, and spread batter in it evenly. Bake cornbread in the middle of the oven for 15 minutes, or until top is pale golden and the sides begin to pull away from the edges of the pan.
4. Allow cornbread to cool for 5 minutes, then turn it out onto a rack. Cut into pieces, and serve hot or at room temperature.

Note: The cornbread is best eaten within a few hours of baking.

Basic Pizza Dough

If you are purchasing your pizza dough rather than making it at home, you can jump to step 4 of this recipe. I think it's much easier to make smaller pizzas rather than a large one, so that is the way this recipe is written. If you want to make larger rounds, or one huge pizza, feel free to do so. This recipe is for the basic dough; follow your pizza recipe for instructions on how long and when to bake it.

Yield: 4 (8-inch) pizzas | **Active time:** 15 minutes | **Start to finish:** 50 minutes, including 30 minutes for rising

> 1 ($\frac{1}{4}$-ounce) package active dry yeast
> $\frac{3}{4}$ cup lukewarm (100–110°F) water
> 3 cups all-purpose flour, divided, plus extra for working dough
> 1 teaspoon salt
> 1 tablespoon honey
> 2 tablespoons olive oil

1. Combine yeast, water, and $\frac{1}{4}$ cup flour in a mixing bowl, and whisk well to dissolve yeast. Set aside for 5 minutes, or until mixture begins to become foamy.
2. Transfer mixture to the bowl of a standard electric mixer fitted with the paddle attachment. Add remaining flour, salt, honey, and olive oil, and beat at low speed until flour is incorporated to form a soft dough.
3. Transfer dough to a lightly floured surface and knead for 5 minutes, or until smooth. Place dough in a greased deep mixing bowl and allow dough to rest, covered with a clean, dry towel, for 30–40 minutes, or until doubled in bulk.
4. Divide dough into 4 equal parts, and roll each piece into a smooth, tight ball. Place balls on a flat dish, covered with a damp towel, and refrigerate if not cooking immediately.
5. Lightly flour a work surface, and using the fleshy part of your fingertips, flatten each dough ball into a circle, approximately 6 inches in diameter, leaving outer edge thicker than center. Dust dough on both sides with flour. Lift dough from the work surface and gently stretch

the edges, working clockwise, to form dough circles that are ¼ inch thick. Sprinkle additional flour on pizza paddles or baking sheets, and place pizza circles on top of flour. Lightly rub a long sheet of plastic wrap with flour, then invert loosely over pizza rounds and let them stand to puff slightly while preheating the oven, 10–20 minutes.

Note: The dough balls can be made up to 6 hours in advance, and refrigerated. Allow dough to sit at room temperature for 1 hour before baking.

Variations: Your dough can be plain or fancy:
- Add 3 tablespoons of chopped fresh herbs to the basic pizza dough.
- Add ¼ cup freshly grated Parmesan cheese to the basic pizza dough.
- To make whole-wheat dough, substitute 1 cup whole-wheat flour for 1 cup of the all-purpose flour.
- Pizza dough can also be used to make calzones, which are stuffed Italian sandwiches. Roll out the dough as specified and then layer filling on half of it. Fold the dough over to form a half moon, crimping the edges to seal in the filling. Bake the calzone at 400°F for 25–30 minutes, or until browned and crisp.

Basic French Bread

This easy recipe is foolproof; I've been making it for years. For a yeast bread it's also relatively quick to make.

Yield: 1 loaf | **Active time:** 20 minutes | **Start to finish:** 3 hours

> 1 (¼-ounce) package active dry yeast
> 1¼ cups water (110–115°F)
> 1 teaspoon granulated sugar
> 3 cups bread flour, divided
> 1½ teaspoons kosher salt
> 3 tablespoons cornmeal

1. Combine yeast, water, sugar, and ¼ cup flour in a mixing bowl, and whisk well to dissolve yeast. Set aside for 5 minutes, or until mixture begins to become foamy.

2. Transfer mixture to the bowl of a standard electric mixer fitted with the paddle attachment. Add remaining flour and salt, and beat a low speed until flour is incorporated to form a soft dough.

3. Place the dough hook on the mixer, and knead dough at medium speed for 2 minutes. Raise the speed to high, and knead for an additional 3–4 minutes, or until dough is springy and elastic. If kneading by hand, it will take about 10–12 minutes. Oil a mixing bowl, and add dough, turning it to make sure top is oiled. Cover bowl with a sheet of plastic wrap, and place it in a warm spot for 1–2 hours, or until dough is doubled in bulk.

4. Lightly oil a baking sheet and sprinkle the center with cornmeal. Punch down dough, and transfer it to a floured surface. Roll or pat dough into a 12x6-inch rectangle. Roll dough up tightly from the 12-inch side; shape dough so that ends come to a point. Transfer dough to prepared baking sheet, placing seam down. Cover dough with plastic wrap, and let rise until doubled in bulk, about 45–60 minutes.

5. Preheat the oven to 425°F, and place a low metal pan on the bottom of the oven as it preheats.

6. Slash top of bread in 3 places with a sharp knife. Add ¾ cup water to the hot pan in the oven. Bake bread for 20–30 minutes, or until it is golden brown and sounds hollow when tapped.

7. Remove the pan from the oven, and cool bread on a rack.

Note: The recipe can be doubled.

The right temperature is necessary for dough to rise. There are some tricks to creating a warm enough temperature in a cold kitchen. Set a foil-covered electric heating pad on low, and put the bowl of dough on the foil; put the bowl in the dishwasher and set it for just the drying cycle; put the bowl in your gas oven to benefit from the warmth of the pilot light; put the bowl in any cold oven over a large pan of boiling-hot water.

Basic Focaccia

Italian focaccia, pronounced *foe-KAH-cha,* is one of the world's great nibble foods, as well as being flat so it's perfect for splitting into a sandwich. **Yield:** 1 loaf (11x17 inches)| **Active time:** 20 minutes | **Start to finish:** 3½ hours

3 (¼-ounce) packages active dry yeast

2¼ cups water (110–115°F)

1 tablespoon granulated sugar

7 cups all-purpose flour, divided, plus additional if necessary

½ cup extra-virgin olive oil, divided

1 tablespoon kosher salt

Coarse salt and freshly ground black for sprinkling

1. Combine yeast, water, sugar, and ¼ cup flour in a mixing bowl, and whisk well to dissolve yeast. Set aside for 5 minutes, or until mixture begins to become foamy.

2. Transfer mixture to the bowl of a standard electric mixer fitted with the paddle attachment. Add ⅓ cup oil, remaining flour, and salt, and beat at low speed until flour is incorporated to form a soft dough.

3. Place the dough hook on the mixer, and knead dough at medium speed for 2 minutes. Raise the speed to high, and knead for an additional 3–4 minutes, or until dough forms a soft ball and is springy. If kneading by hand, it will take about 10–12 minutes. Oil a mixing bowl, and add dough, turning it to make sure top is oiled. Cover bowl with a sheet of plastic wrap, and place it in a warm spot for 1–2 hours, or until dough is doubled in bulk.

4. Preheat the oven to 450°F, and oil an 11x17-inch baking sheet. Gently press dough into the prepared pan; allow dough to rest 5 minutes if difficult to work with. Cover the pan with a sheet of oiled plastic wrap, and let rise in a warm place until doubled in bulk, about 30 minutes.

5. Make indentations in dough at 1-inch intervals with oiled fingertips. Drizzle with remaining oil, and sprinkle with coarse salt and pepper. Bake in lower third of oven until deep golden on top and pale golden on bottom, 25–30 minutes. Transfer bread to a rack and serve warm or at room temperature.

Note: This amount of dough is about the maximum that a home standard mixer can make, so the recipe cannot be increased. However, it can be made smaller proportionally.

Variations: The reason why focaccia is such a great nibble food is that there's so much surface area that can be flavored. Try these recipe additions; all are added before the bread is baked:

- Sprinkle the top with ¼ cup of a chopped fresh herb such as rosemary, basil, oregano, or some combination.
- Spread sautéed onions or fennel across the top of the dough before baking.
- Sprinkle the top with ¾ cup freshly grated Parmesan cheese.
- Sprinkle the top with ¾ cup chopped black oil-cured olives.
- Soak 4 garlic cloves, peeled and minced, in the olive oil for 2 hours before making the dough. Either strain and discard garlic, or use it if you really like things garlicky.

No-Knead White Bread

Starting in about 2007, many cookbook authors and food writers began breaking through the hesitancy of making yeast bread by formulating recipes that would succeed *without* the elbow grease necessary for proper kneading. I played around with numbers of these; some were much more successful than others. Here's one, based on a recipe by Mark Bittman from the *New York Times* that I like a lot.

Yield: 1 loaf | **Active time:** 10 minutes | **Start to finish:** 5½ hours

> 1 packet (¼ ounce) instant yeast
> 1½ cups water (110–115°F)
> 2 teaspoons granulated sugar
> 3 cups bread flour, divided
> 2 teaspoons kosher salt

1. Combine yeast, water, sugar, and ¼ cup flour in a mixing bowl, and whisk well to dissolve yeast. Set aside for 5 minutes, or until mixture begins to become foamy.
2. Add remaining flour and salt, and stir well; the dough will be loose and shaggy. Cover the bowl loosely with plastic wrap. Set bowl in a warm location, and allow dough to rise for 4 hours.
3. Scrape dough out of the mixing bowl, and place it on a well-oiled surface. Using oiled hands, form the dough into a ball, and cover it loosely with plastic wrap. Allow dough to rest for 30 minutes.
4. Preheat the oven to 450°F, and place a 4–6-quart roasting pan in the oven as it preheats. Carefully place dough ball into the hot pan, cover the pan with its lid or a sheet of aluminum foil, and bake bread for 30 minutes. Uncover the pan, and bake for an additional 20–30 minutes, or until bread is brown and sounds hollow when tapped.
5. Remove the pan from the oven, and cool bread on a rack.

Note: This recipe can be doubled successfully.

Variations: Because the dough is soft, many additions can be stirred in at the time the dough is formed into a ball:
- Add 2 tablespoons of a chopped herb, such as rosemary, oregano, or dill.
- Add ½ cup chopped oil-cured black olives.
- Add ¼ cup freshly grated Parmesan cheese or grated cheddar cheese.

Basic Pie Crust

Another bakery item that costs very little to make at home is pie crust, and even if you never make a traditional pie, knowing how to make pie crust is important. It could lead to spicy empanadas or a savory quiche for lunch. Pie crust is essentially flour and fat, mixed with a little salt and water. The method remains constant; what changes is the proportion of ingredients.

Yield: Varies | **Active time:** 15 minutes | **Start to finish:** 15 minutes

Proportions for Pie Crust

Size	Flour	Salt	Butter	Ice Water
8–10-inch single	1⅓ cups	½ tsp	½ cup	3–4 tblsp
8–9-inch double	2 cups	¾ tsp	¾ cup	5–6 tblsp
10-inch double	2⅔ cups	1 tsp	1 cup	7–8 tblsp

1. Combine flour and salt in a medium mixing bowl. Cut butter into cubes the size of lima beans, and cut into flour using a pastry blender, two knives, or your fingertips until mixture forms pea-sized chunks. This can also be done in a food processor fitted with a steel blade using on-and-off pulsing.

2. Sprinkle mixture with water, 1 tablespoon at a time. Toss lightly with fork until dough will form a ball. If using a food processor, process until mixture holds together when pressed between two fingers; if it is processed until it forms a ball, too much water has been added.

3. Depending on whether it is to be a 1- or 2-crust pie, form dough into 1 or 2 (5–6-inch) "pancakes." Flour pancake lightly on both sides, and, if time permits, refrigerate dough before rolling it to allow more even distribution of the moisture.

4. Dough can be rolled either between 2 sheets of waxed paper or inside a lightly floured plastic bag. Use the former method for pie crust dough that will be used for formed pastries such as empanadas, and the latter to make circles suitable for lining or topping a pie pan. For a round circle, make sure dough starts out in the center of the bag, and then keep turning it in ¼ turns until the circle is 1 inch larger in diameter than the inverted pie plate. Either remove the top sheet of wax paper or cut the bag open on the sides. Then either

begin to cut out shapes or invert the dough into a pie plate, pressing it into the bottom and up the sides, and extending the dough 1 inch beyond the edge of the pie plate.

5. If you want to partially or totally bake the pie shell before filling, prick the bottom and sides with a fork, press in a sheet of wax paper, and fill the pie plate with dried beans, rice, or the metal pie stones sold in cookware stores. Place in a 375ºF oven for 10–15 minutes. The shell is now partially baked. To complete baking, remove the weights and wax paper, and bake an additional 15–20 minutes, or until golden brown. Otherwise, fill pie shell. If you want a double crust pie, roll out the second half of the dough the same way you did the first half, and invert it over the top, crimping the edges and cutting in some steam vents with the tip of a sharp knife.

Note: The crust can be prepared up to 3 days in advance and refrigerated, tightly covered. Also, both dough "pancakes" and rolled-out sheets can be frozen for up to 3 months.

Variations: Once you've made the dough, you can dress up your pie. Here are different ways.

- To create a fluted edge: Trim the pastry ½ inch beyond the edge of the plate, and fold under to make a plump pastry edge. Place your index finger on the inside of the pastry edge, right thumb and index finger on the outside. Pinch the pastry into V shapes, and repeat the pinching to sharpen the design.
- For an easy lattice crust: Cut ½–¾-inch-wide strips of pie crust, using a pastry wheel or knife. Lay the strips across the pie in one direction, then in the other. Do not weave; however, fold edge of the bottom crust over the pastry strips and flute.
- For a shiny crust: Blend 1 egg yolk with 1 tablespoon milk or water. Brush over the top of the pie before baking.

Basic Crumb Crust

Crumb crusts are easy to make, and much less expensive than purchasing them ready-made in the supermarket. While graham cracker is traditional for sweetened cheese pies, key lime pies, and fruit pies, you can also use chocolate, vanilla, or any plain unfilled cookie to make a crust.

Yield: 1 (9-inch pie) | **Active time:** 10 minutes | **Start to finish:** 10 minutes

30 graham crackers or 2 cups graham cracker crumbs
6 tablespoons (¾ stick) unsalted butter, melted
2 tablespoons granulated sugar
½ teaspoon ground cinnamon (optional)

1. If using graham crackers, crush them into crumbs by breaking them into small pieces and chopping them in a food processor fitted with the steel blade using on-and-off pulsing, or place the pieces in a heavy resealable plastic bag and crush to crumbs with the bottom of a small skillet.
2. Combine crumbs, butter, sugar, and cinnamon, if using, in a mixing bowl, and mix well.
3. Spread mixture into bottom and up sides of the pie plate, pushing it firmly into place. Follow recipe directions for when to bake crust.

Note: The crust can be prepared for baking up to 2 days in advance and refrigerated, tightly covered.

Cream Puffs

The dough is called *pâte a choux* in classic French cooking, and it's a useful dough to learn how to bake. You can make big cream puffs or small puffs; they can be sweet and filled with ice cream or berries, or they can be savory and served as hors d'oeuvres filled with a mousse.

Yield: 3 dozen small puffs or 1 dozen large puffs | **Active time:** 30 minutes | **Start to finish:** 1¼ hours

> 1 cup water
> 6 tablespoons (¾ stick) unsalted butter
> 2 teaspoons granulated sugar (if making puffs for sweet fillings only)
> ½ teaspoon salt
> ¼ teaspoon pure vanilla extract (if making puffs for sweet fillings only)
> ¾ cup all-purpose flour
> 5 large eggs, divided

1. Preheat the oven to 425°F, and grease two cookie sheets.
2. Combine water, butter, sugar, salt, and vanilla in a saucepan, and bring to a boil over medium-high heat, stirring occasionally. Remove the pan from the heat, and add flour all at once. Using a wooden paddle or wide wooden spoon, beat flour into the liquid until it is smooth. Then place the saucepan over high heat and beat mixture constantly for 1 to 2 minutes, until it forms a mass that leaves the sides of the pan and begins to film the bottom of the pot.
3. Transfer mixture to a food processor fitted with the steel blade. Add 4 of the eggs, 1 at a time, beating well between each addition and scraping the sides of the work bowl between each addition. This can also be done by hand.
4. Scrape dough into a pastry bag fitted with an unfluted tip. For small puffs, pipe mounds 1 inch in diameter and ½ inch high onto the baking sheets, allowing 1½ inches between puffs. For large puffs, make the mounds 2½ inches wide and no more than one inch high. Or pipe mixture into lines of these dimensions for éclair shape.

5. Beat remaining egg with a pinch of salt, and brush only tops of dough mounds with a small pastry brush or rub gently with a finger dipped in the egg wash. (Be careful not to drip egg wash onto the baking sheet or egg may prevent dough from puffing.)

6. Bake small puffs for 20–25 minutes, or until puffs are golden brown and crusty to the touch. Remove the pans from the oven, and using the tip of a paring knife, cut a slit in the side of each puff to allow the steam to escape. Turn off the oven, and place the baked puffs back into the oven with the oven door ajar for 10 minutes to finish crisping them. Remove them from the oven and place on a wire rack to cool.

   For large puffs, bake at 425°F for 20 minutes, and then reduce the heat to 375°F and bake an additional 10–15 minutes. Crisp them as above. (With large puffs there is a chance that there is still some damp dough in the center. After crisping, split large puffs completely with a serrated knife, and pull out any damp dough. Cool puffs in halves rather than whole.)

Note: The puffs can be made up to 1 day in advance and kept at room temperature.

Variation: Ah, once you can make the puffs you can do almost anything. Try this variation:

- For a cream puff ring, called Paris Breast in classic French cooking: Flour the greased baking sheet, and draw a 10-inch circle on the baking sheet, using a pot lid or platter as a guide. Pipe two thick lines side by side, using the circle as a guide, and then nestle one line into the crevice between the two. Bake for 20 minutes at 425°F, and then 25 minutes at 350°F. Split, pull out the damp dough, and crisp as described above.

If puffs become soggy, they can be crisped by placing them in a 350°F oven for 5–7 minutes. For large puffs, crisp the halves apart with the inside part up on both halves.

Appendix A:
Metric Conversion Tables

The scientifically precise calculations needed for baking are not necessary when cooking conventionally. The tables in this appendix are designed for general cooking. If making conversions for baking, grab your calculator and compute the exact figure.

CONVERTING OUNCES TO GRAMS
The numbers in the following table are approximate. To reach the exact quantity of grams, multiply the number of ounces by 28.35.

Ounces	Grams
1 ounce	30 grams
2 ounces	60 grams
3 ounces	85 grams
4 ounces	115 grams
5 ounces	140 grams
6 ounces	180 grams
7 ounces	200 grams
8 ounces	225 grams
9 ounces	250 grams
10 ounces	285 grams
11 ounces	300 grams
12 ounces	340 grams
13 ounces	370 grams
14 ounces	400 grams
15 ounces	425 grams
16 ounces	450 grams

CONVERTING QUARTS TO LITERS

The numbers in the following table are approximate. To reach the exact amount of liters, multiply the number of quarts by 0.95.

Quarts	Liter
1 cup (1/4 quart)	1/4 liter
1 pint (1/2 quart)	1/2 liter
1 quart	1 liter
2 quarts	2 liters
2 1/2 quarts	2 1/2 liters
3 quarts	2 3/4 liters
4 quarts	3 3/4 liters
5 quarts	4 3/4 liters
6 quarts	5 1/2 liters
7 quarts	6 1/2 liters
8 quarts	7 1/2 liters

CONVERTING POUNDS TO GRAMS AND KILOGRAMS

The numbers in the following table are approximate. To reach the exact quantity of grams, multiply the number of pounds by 453.6.

Pounds	Grams; Kilograms
1 pound	450 grams
1 1/2 pounds	675 grams
2 pounds	900 grams
2 1/2 pounds	1,125 grams; 1 1/4 kilograms
3 pounds	1,350 grams
3 1/2 pounds	1,500 grams; 1 1/2 kilograms
4 pounds	1,800 grams
4 1/2 pounds	2 kilograms
5 pounds	2 1/4 kilograms
5 1/2 pounds	2 1/2 kilograms
6 pounds	2 3/4 kilograms
6 1/2 pounds	3 kilograms
7 pounds	3 1/4 kilograms
7 1/2 pounds	3 1/2 kilograms
8 pounds	3 3/4 kilograms

CONVERTING FAHRENHEIT TO CELSIUS

The numbers in the following table are approximate. To reach the exact temperature, subtract 32 from the Fahrenheit reading, multiply the number by 5, and then divide by 9.

Degrees Fahrenheit	Degrees Celsius
170°F	77°C
180°F	82°C
190°F	88°C
200°F	95°C
225°F	110°C
250°F	120°C
300°F	150°C
325°F	165°C
350°F	180°C
375°F	190°C
400°F	205°C
425°F	220°C
450°F	230°C
475°F	245°C
500°F	260°C

CONVERTING INCHES TO CENTIMETERS

The numbers in the following table are approximate. To reach the exact number of centimeters, multiply the number of inches by 2.54.

Inches	Centimeters
½ inch	1.5 centimeters
1 inch	2.5 centimeters
2 inches	5 centimeters
3 inches	8 centimeters
4 inches	10 centimeters
5 inches	13 centimeters
6 inches	15 centimeters
7 inches	18 centimeters
8 inches	20 centimeters
9 inches	23 centimeters
10 inches	25 centimeters
11 inches	28 centimeters
12 inches	30 centimeters

Appendix B:
Table of Weights and Measures of Common Ingredients

Food	Quantity	Yield
Apples	1 pound	2½–3 cups sliced
Avocado	1 pound	1 cup mashed
Bananas	1 medium	1 cup sliced
Bell peppers	1 pound	3–4 cups sliced
Blueberries	1 pound	3⅓ cups
Butter	¼ pound (1 stick)	8 tablespoons
Cabbage	1 pound	4 cups packed shredded
Carrots	1 pound	3 cups diced or sliced
Chocolate, morsels	12 ounces	2 cups
Chocolate, bulk	1 ounce	3 tablespoons grated
Cocoa powder	1 ounce	¼ cup
Coconut, flaked	7 ounces	2½ cups
Cream	½ pint (1 cup)	2 cups whipped
Cream cheese	8 ounces	1 cup
Flour	1 pound	4 cups
Lemons	1 medium	3 tablespoons juice
Lemons	1 medium	2 teaspoons zest
Milk	1 quart	4 cups
Molasses	12 ounces	1½ cups
Mushrooms	1 pound	5 cups sliced
Onions	1 medium	½ cup chopped
Peaches	1 pound	2 cups sliced
Peanuts	5 ounces	1 cup
Pecans	6 ounces	1½ cups
Pineapple	1 medium	3 cups diced
Potatoes	1 pound	3 cups sliced
Raisins	1 pound	3 cups
Rice	1 pound	2 to 2½ cups raw
Spinach	1 pound	¾ cup cooked
Squash, summer	1 pound	3½ cups sliced
Strawberries	1 pint	1½ cups sliced

Food	Quantity	Yield
Sugar, brown	1 pound	2¼ cups, packed
Sugar, confectioners'	1 pound	4 cups
Sugar, granulated	1 pound	2¼ cups
Tomatoes	1 pound	1½ cups pulp
Walnuts	4 ounces	1 cup

TABLE OF LIQUID MEASUREMENTS

Dash	=	less than ⅛ teaspoon
3 teaspoons	=	1 tablespoon
2 tablespoons	=	1 ounce
8 tablespoons	=	½ cup
2 cups	=	1 pint
1 quart	=	2 pints
1 gallon	=	4 quarts

Index